SUNDAY
Throughout
the Week

Gaynell Cronin

SUNDAY Throughout the Week

Ave Maria Press
Notre Dame, Indiana 46556-0428

Acknowledgments

Excerpts from *The Jerusalem Bible,* copyright © 1966 by Darton, Longman & Todd, Ltd. and Doubleday & Company, Inc. All scriptural texts are from this bible version unless otherwise noted.

Excerpts from the English translation of *Rite of Baptism for Children* © 1969, International Committee on English in the Liturgy, Inc. (ICEL); excerpts from the English translation of *Rite of Anointing and Pastoral Care of the Sick* © 1973, ICEL; excerpts from the English translation of *The Roman Missal* © 1973, ICEL; excerpts from the English translation of *Rite of Christian Initiation of Adults* © 1974, ICEL. All rights reserved.

**The weekly entries for *Sunday Throughout the Week*
may be reproduced in parish bulletins.**

Contents

Special Celebrations (ABC Cycles)

Sundays Throughout the Year

(The B Cycle begins in late November, 1981; the C Cycle begins in late November, 1982; the A Cycle begins in late November, 1983. This pattern continues throughout subsequent years.)

Author's Introduction

In our family my mother and father had a photograph album for each child. On rainy days, and there were many in New Orleans, my brother, sister and I would slowly go through each page of our book. Some events of our early years we really couldn't remember, but our parents and relatives often told us the story surrounding each photo. We never tired of hearing the same story over and over again. The photographs offered not only a reminder of past events but also provided an experience in the present of listening to the word of another. We treasured those stories and still remember them today through our photograph albums.

There are other stories that we treasured, stories of what God had done for us and continues to do, stories of what Jesus said and did, stories of what we are called to be and do through the Spirit as God's people. For years our family made symbols for favorite stories and characters from the Old and New Testaments: a rainbow for Noah, a cloud for the Transfiguration, loaves and fishes for the feeding of the 5,000. We loved displaying these symbols and being reminded of the stories they represented.

The traditions of the photograph album and the use of symbols to represent treasured stories from the bible were welcomed by our own children. We too became a storytelling family. At first we made signs randomly for different scripture stories; then, led by the children's enthusiasm, we began to make a symbol each week for the gospel we heard at Sunday Mass. While making the symbol, we found ourselves talking about the lesson and deciding on a particular way to live that lesson during the week. The children delighted in making their own prayers at the dinner table, prayers that spoke of the lesson or asked for help in living the message of Jesus. But the symbols that we made and posted in our home were the heart of our storytelling experience. Symbols help the memory. Like the photos in our album, they recall not only the words of God but also the experience we had in listening to those words and living them.

One thing I have discovered with delight is that when we bring the Good News home, it not only fills our own home and hearts, but it overflows to others. One day I heard loud, happy voices in the kitchen. Challenged by her sister, one of our daughters was telling some neighborhood children the story behind each of the different symbols posted in our kitchen. Another daughter kept a tally of the ones she remembered. Symbols! What simple yet effective tools for remembering and teaching the word of God! It was out of that experience that *Sunday Throughout the Week* was born.

And so, to all those people in the Bordes photograph albums, particularly my mother and father, Rick and my sister Bonnie and their children, Arlyss and my brother Barry and their children, thank you for wonderful memories. To my husband, Jim, and our children Claire, Meaghan, James and Maura—the very special people in the Cronin photograph albums—thank you for the life we share. As a family we, with our parish of Holy Name of Mary (particularly Pat O'Neill, typist and affirmer) celebrate and continue to welcome the word of God into our lives and to live that word in joy throughout the year.

—Gaynell Cronin

How to Use This Book

The significance of *Sunday Throughout the Week*

"The parish Sunday Mass is the community celebration which reflects
and shapes the lives of parishioners."

(a.134 NCD)

In the Sunday liturgy the story of what has made us and sustained us is told over and over again. This shared experience makes us one. All parish activity is directed toward the liturgy; all parish life flows from it. The worshipping community gathers on Sunday for common worship. These gathered people represent all ages and backgrounds. They come to celebrate together the presence of God in their lives, to receive his life and to listen to his word. And then they go out to bring the Good News home to their families and their communities.

... catechesis ... prepares people for full and active participation in
liturgy and at the same time flows from liturgy, inasmuch as, reflecting
upon the community's experience of worship, it seeks to relate them
to daily life and to growth in faith.

(a.113 NCD)

Sunday Throughout the Week offers us, as members of the faith community, the opportunity to prepare for the Sunday liturgy by reading the gospel prayerfully before attending Mass. Then, with open ears and hearts, we can welcome the word which has already taken root in us when we hear it proclaimed by the priest. From our experience in a worshipping community we can then *reflect* upon the word we have heard and begin to live it—*talking, doing* and *praying*—in our daily lives. With the weekly addition of a symbol to represent that experience—either on our SUNDAY THROUGHOUT THE YEAR banner or posted in our home or classroom—we see a growth in faith through welcoming and living the word of God.

The structure of *Sunday Throughout the Week*

Sunday Throughout the Week is based on the liturgical year. Four special celebrations—Christmas, Epiphany, Easter and Pentecost—have been placed in a separate section at the beginning of the book. There were two reasons for this: first, the gospel on these feasts is the same in all the Cycles; second, most families have their own traditions (and symbols) for these occasions.

The remainder of the book is divided into three sections: Cycle A, Cycle B and Cycle C. Each cycle follows the church calendar, beginning with the 1st Sunday of Advent and continuing through the Solemnity of Christ the King. Dates throughout the 1980s have been printed on each weekly selection for ease in locating the appropriate reading for the week.

Each weekly section in *Sunday Throughout the Week* consists of four parts:

Reflecting offers a simple commentary or meditation on one of the readings, usually the gospel.

Talking offers questions, statements and value completions that provide a basis for family or group discussion.

Doing provides projects for family or group participation. One activity (Doing #2) is always that of making a scripture symbol. This symbol should be displayed in the home, school or parish. A SUNDAY THROUGHOUT THE YEAR banner (see below) is an effective means of displaying these symbols.

Praying offers group prayer, sometimes accompanied by a ritual gesture or blessing.

A SUNDAY THROUGHOUT THE YEAR banner

This banner is an excellent way to show the growth in faith that is experienced by living the Good News of Jesus which is proclaimed throughout each of the cycles. Across the top of a piece of cloth or a sturdy piece of cardboard, place the words "Sunday Throughout the Year." Each week add a scripture symbol (see Doing #2 in each selection) to the banner. At the end of the cycle you will have the whole story, in symbols, of God's word to his people. A picture of a completed banner introduces each of the cycles in this book. The banner can be used effectively in the home, in the classroom or school, or in the parish.

Home—In the home the banner stands as a reminder of the Good News which the family is trying to live. It serves as a sign that the Good News is part of the very structure of the home.

School—Catechists can teach through the weekly scripture symbol which is placed on the banner in the school or classroom. Through these signs they can encourage the students to review their knowledge and understanding of the stories and sayings of Jesus.

Parish—Display the banner in the church. During the opening procession of one of the Sunday Masses, present the weekly symbol and attach it to the banner.

Ways to use *Sunday Throughout the Week*

The heart of the *Sunday Throughout the Week* experience is, of course, the family. Bringing God's gift of his word home and living it supported and affirmed by a loving family is ideal. However, by using *Sunday Throughout the Week*, a teacher can bring the Good News "home" to his or her classroom; a person in pastoral ministry to his or her parish. Preparation for the Sunday liturgy gives unity to family life, school life and parish life. Living God's word during the week gives oneness to the family of God.

Sunday Throughout the Week can be used as a complete program of *Reflecting, Talking, Doing* and *Praying* or it can be adapted to the needs of the particular home, classroom or parish. The selections can, for example, be easily distributed for use throughout a parish by being inserted each week in the parish bulletin. CCD and parochial school classes, family programs, meetings of parish organizations, parish renewal programs, all can use *Praying* or *Reflecting* to begin or conclude their gatherings, *Doing* as a source of activities, and *Talking* for discussion starters. Some parishes find the *Reflecting* and the *Praying* sections useful for prayer services. Some groups emphasize *Talking*; for example, one parish has children complete the value statements and uses the responses as the basis for a dialogue homily. Confirmation classes in another parish keep a weekly journal by completing the *Talking* sections and make the scripture symbols with their families.

Sunday Throughout the Week will help you bring the Good News home to your family, your classroom or your parish in whatever way works best for you!

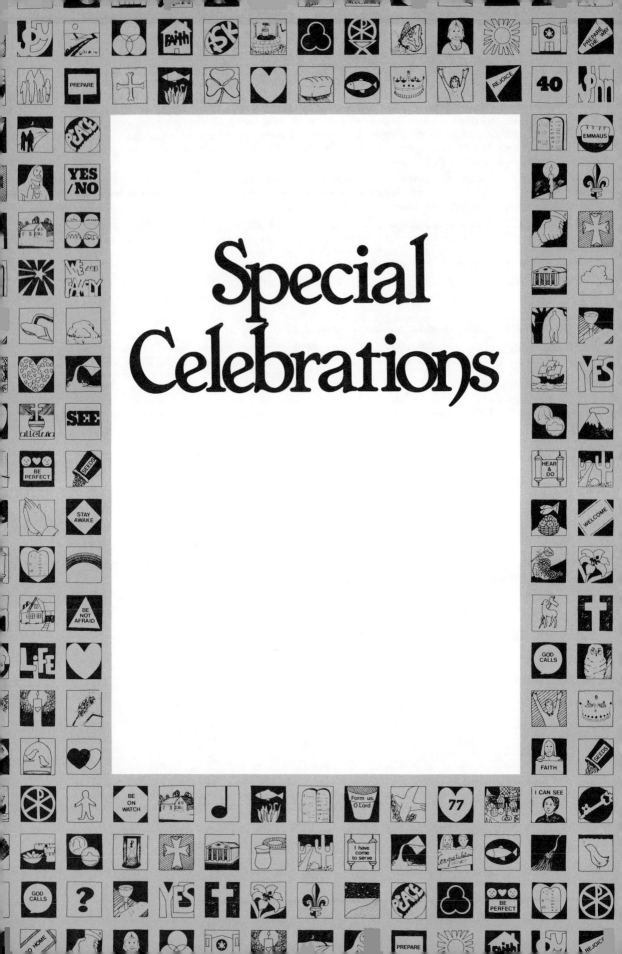

Special Celebrations

Christmas (Jn 1:1-18)

REFLECTING

All of life welcomes Jesus. On the birthday of Jesus, all of life rejoices. How wonderful it is to celebrate new life!

This is the day the Lord has made! This is the fullness of time. This is the day to remember the wonderful things God has done for us, a day to remember his gift of love to us. God so loved us that he gifted us with his son.

Today's gospel, the prologue of St. John, is the traditional gospel of Christmas Day. Many people think that this prologue may have been an early Christian hymn. Through it we express the mystery and heart of our faith: Christ is God made man.

Jesus came to show us how to love with a generous heart. How will we live the story of Jesus? How will we share the joy of his presence with us now and forever? How will we celebrate his life as light within us?

As members of a family, let us give ourselves as gifts to God and to one another. Let us live as gifted people. Let us pray the words of Isaiah:

> The people that walked in darkness
> has seen a great light;
>
> For there is a child born for us,
> a son given to us
>
> and this is the name they give him:
> Wonder-Counsellor, Mighty-God,
> Eternal-Father, Prince of Peace (*Is 9:1, 5-6*).
>
> *Thank you, God.*

TALKING

1. Talk about Jesus as God's gift to you. Consider: What you are is God's gift to you, what you become is your gift to God. Discuss ways you can live and give yourself as a gift on this Christmas day.

2. Talk about the birth of Jesus. Who welcomed him? How was his birth celebrated? What effects does his birth have in your life and the life of the world?

3. Share your answers:
   I walk as a child of light by _____.
   My gift to Jesus is _____.
   To celebrate new life, I will _____.

DOING

1. Write a Christmas prayer of thanksgiving to be said at your Christmas dinner. Make place cards for this meal of celebration.

2. Make your weekly scripture symbol—a Chi-Rho over a crib. Place it in your home or on your SUNDAY THROUGHOUT THE YEAR banner.

PRAYING

(If you have a manger, process with the figure of the baby Jesus as you sing "O Come, All Ye Faithful." Stand before the manger, hold the baby Jesus, and pray:)

God,
You love us so much that you send your Son as a gift to us. He is the light of the world, our light. Praise to you, God. Glory for the birthday of Jesus.

(Sing "Silent Night" as you place the figure of the infant Jesus in the manger.)

Epiphany (Mt 2:1-12)

REFLECTING

The feast of the Epiphany celebrates God manifesting himself in Christ to all people. The Magi represent the Gentiles, all of us, and come with gifts to honor this newborn king. On this feast we see Jesus as Messiah coming to bring salvation to all people.

Epiphany is a Greek word meaning "manifestation." In ancient times the term referred to an official visit by a king or queen, a public showing to the people. As God showed himself to us through Jesus on this day, so we are to show the presence of God to others by our own lives.

It is said that a single star led the way for the Magi, these travelers from the East. Their gifts of gold, frankincense and myrrh represent products of the East. Whether these elements of the story are factual or not, the truth they represent is important for each of us: In Jesus, God reveals his plan of salvation for all people.

Each of us is called to follow our star, to search for truth and love in Jesus. We are all on a journey. To everyone we meet we reflect the light of God. We become an epiphany for others so that together we can honor Jesus as our king.

TALKING

1. As a family discuss ways you can be a light to others.
2. Reflect on the lyrics of "The Impossible Dream" from *Man of La Mancha*. Why is it sometimes so difficult to follow our star?
3. Share your answers:
   To follow my star, I will _____.
   One of the best ways to show Jesus to others is by _____.
   The gift I bring to Jesus is _____.

DOING

1. While singing "We Three Kings of Orient Are," process through your home with statues of the Wise Men and place them in your manger scene.

2. Make your weekly scripture symbol—a star. Place it in your home or on your SUNDAY THROUGHOUT THE YEAR banner.

PRAYING

God,
Thank you for showing Jesus to all of us. As the light of the star revealed Jesus, so let us become a light that reveals him to others.

Leader: Arise and shine out, our light has come.
All: Arise and shine out, our light has come.
Leader: The glory of the Lord shines upon you.
All: The glory of the Lord shines upon you.
Leader: Shout the praises of the Lord.
All: Shout the praises of the Lord.

Easter (Jn 20:1-9)

REFLECTING

Spring! New flowers, free-running water, sunny skies! Our winter has passed and our spring, our new life, has arrived!

This feast of the Resurrection is the greatest feast of the church year. The gospel today is the original "Good News": Jesus of Nazareth, crucified, is risen and is present with us.

Can you imagine the astonishment of Mary Magdalene when she arrived and found the tomb empty? As she ran to find Peter and John, she must have been troubled; she was concerned that some robbers had come in the night.

Peter and John ran to the tomb. John arrived first but waited for Peter to enter the tomb first. It is amazing that he held his excitement and waited! Following Peter, Mary and John walked into the tomb. Together they saw the clothes and the head garment, rolled and placed neatly apart. They were filled with awe.

There is an emphasis in this gospel on vision, on seeing. Peter, Mary and John *saw*. We have an additional line about John, "He *saw* and *believed*." How quickly would we have been able to see and to believe?

We rejoice today and all days. Alleluia! He is risen! He is among us now! See and believe!

TALKING

1. Recreate the resurrection scene by sharing your insights on the feelings of Mary, John and Peter as they saw the empty tomb. Place yourself in the story. Where would you be standing? What would you say?

2. As a family, list all the things and people that give you joy, new hope, new life.

3. Share your answers:
   As a symbol of the Resurrection, I would choose _____.
   If I had seen the empty tomb, I would have felt _____.
   I rejoice when I see _____.

DOING

1. Make or buy a thick candle. With ceremony, place a cross on the candle. Place the Alpha A at the top and the Omega Ω at the bottom as symbols that Christ is the beginning and the end. Place the year on the candle.

2. Make your weekly scripture symbol—a butterfly. Place it in your home or on your SUNDAY THROUGHOUT THE YEAR banner.

PRAYING

Response: Alleluia, Alleluia, Alleluia.

You came, Lord, that we might have new life. You died to give us that new life . . .
You showed us the way to live, the way to die, and the way to live again . . .
You promised that we too will one day rise . . .

There is laughter and shouts of joy because Jesus, our friend and our Lord, has risen! May we always shout his praises . . .

(Sing Acclamation "a" as a family.)
Christ has died, alleluia,
Christ is risen, alleluia,
Christ will come again, alleluia, alleluia.

**Apr 11, 1982 / Apr 3, 1983 / Apr 22, 1984 / Apr 7, 1985 /
Mar 30, 1986 /Apr 19, 1987 / Apr 3, 1988 / Mar 26, 1989**

Pentecost (Jn 20:19-23)

REFLECTING

> Pentecost celebrates the birthday of the church,
> the giving of the Spirit,
> the call to follow the Spirit.
> Pentecost is the celebration of gifts.

Today's first reading (Acts 2:1-11) is set on the 50th day after Passover. Many people have gathered in Jerusalem for the Feast of Weeks. One hundred and twenty of Jesus' disciples are assembled in one place. Together they await the Spirit that Jesus has promised. Imagine the excitement of the disciples as they receive the gifts of the Spirit.

Suddenly, there is a noise like a powerful wind. Tongues of fire appear, part and come to rest on each disciple. Each individual present is "filled with the Spirit." With peace and courage these disciples begin to proclaim the Good News.

We, too, receive the gifts of the Spirit. We should live with a deep, inner joy, knowing that the Spirit is present with us and will give us the strength to be "good news" for others.

TALKING

1. Discuss the seven gifts of the Holy Spirit. Talk about the different people in the world who are using these gifts.

2. How do you recognize the presence of the Spirit in your life? Discuss the notion of gifts and the uniqueness of our individual gifts.

3. Share your answers:
My favorite gift of the seven gifts of the Spirit is _____ because _____.

The gift of the Spirit that seems to be most present in our family is _____.

DOING

1. Share joy with everyone you meet this week. Bring peace, hope and love to others and remember the presence of the Spirit in all of these experiences.

2. Make your weekly scripture symbol—a flame. Place it in your home or on your SUNDAY THROUGHOUT THE YEAR banner.

PRAYING

Dear Holy Spirit,
Enlighten us, protect us, direct us, and govern us. Fill us with the courage to speak the Good News, with peace to live the Good News, and with joy to rejoice in the Good News.

Be in our lives as we leave the life of winter and begin our summer. Help us to renew the face of the earth.

(Thank one another for particular gifts and for using those gifts.)

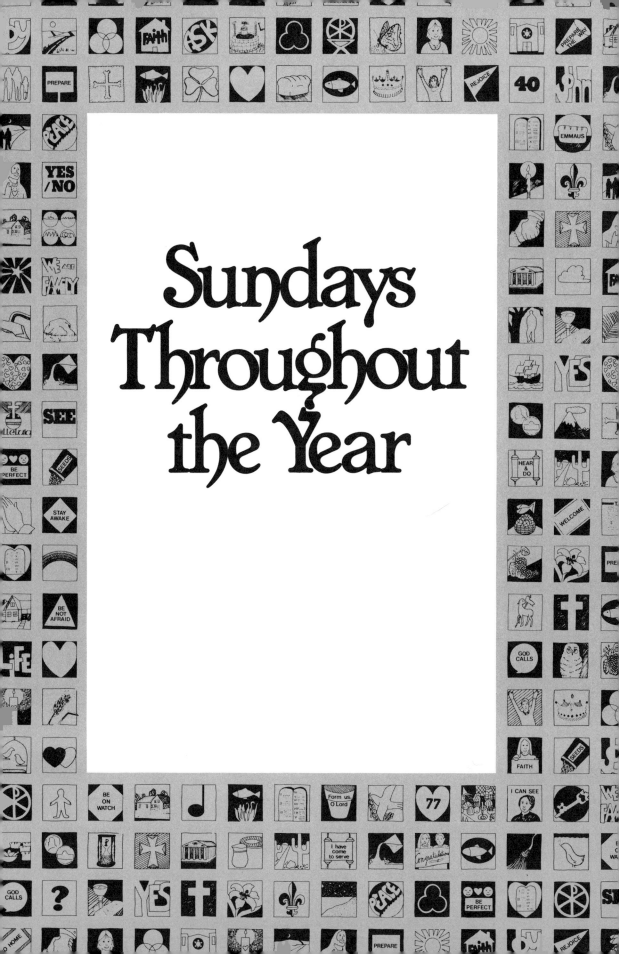

Sundays Throughout the Year

CYCLE A

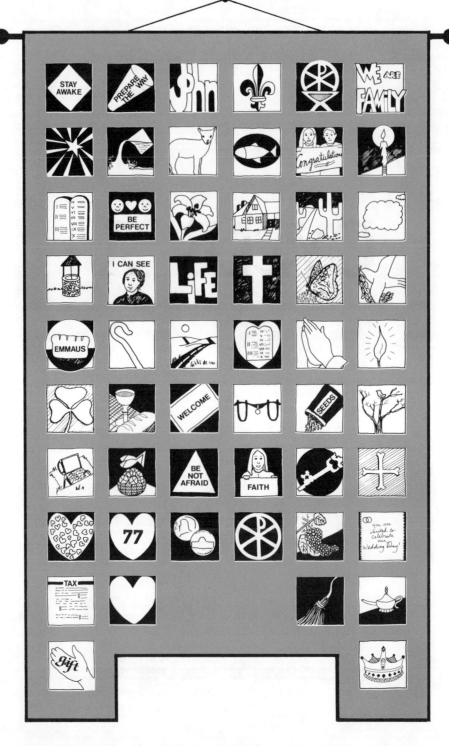

SUNDAY THROUGHOUT THE YEAR Banner—Cycle A

1st Sunday of Advent (Mt 24:37-44)

REFLECTING

Food, house, car, clothes, fame, money, land, parties, business, travel, shopping, ... the list can go on forever.

Sometimes our world distracts us. We become busy with many things, careless and shortsighted in the way we live. Sometimes we live only for the moment, unaware of our past and unconcerned about our future. We become like the people of Noah's day, forgetting God and forgetting we are his people.

This Sunday's gospel asks us to become aware of our need for God. We live aware of our need for food, for security, for companionship, for acceptance. Daily we are reminded of our physical and emotional needs by the media and our own experiences. But how often do we recognize, experience and try to fulfill our deep need and longing for God?

We must welcome God daily in our hearts so that we may stay awake and be prepared for his Second Coming, a coming for which we know not the day or the time. We must stay awake in living our need for God.

We now begin a new liturgical year. Matthew will be our primary gospel writer during this A cycle. This is the season of Advent—a time of wearing violet vestments, a time of preparing for the coming of the Lord at Christmas and his coming in glory at the end of the world. As a family, let us prepare together for Christmas.

TALKING

1. What are the different ways Jesus comes to us in our daily lives? Consider ways to prepare for these comings.
2. We experience different needs at different times in our lives. What is your greatest need right now? How do you try to answer this need?
3. Share your answers:
   To help me remember God's presence in my life, I _____.
   To "stay awake" during Advent, I will _____.

DOING

1. Make an Advent wreath. Place a cup in the center of the wreath. This cup will be used as your "family cup of blessing." You will drink from it at the close of family prayer during Advent.
2. Make a scripture symbol for the week—a "Stay awake" sign. Place it in your home or on your SUNDAY THROUGHOUT THE YEAR banner.

PRAYING

(Fill the cup of blessing. Light one candle of the Advent wreath. Then gather around the Advent wreath and offer the following prayer.)

You are coming, Lord Jesus! With joy and excitement we prepare together for this coming. We light this Advent candle as a sign that we will stay awake to welcome you.

Help us to recognize our need for you in our lives. Let us never be like the people of Noah's day, careless in our living and forgetful of your presence. We drink from our family cup of blessing as a sign that we are one as we prepare for your Christmas coming.

(In silence, pass the cup around to each family member.)

Nov 27, 1983 / Nov 30, 1986

2nd Sunday of Advent (Mt 3:1-12)

REFLECTING

"I am afraid to speak before others. Maybe they will laugh at what I am saying. I don't want to look ridiculous." How often we have said or heard others say these words. It seems to be part of our human nature to need courage in presenting our thoughts before others.

We have a good example of fortitude, courage and fearlessness in the figure of John the Baptist. Clothed in a camel's hair garment, eating grasshoppers and wild honey, living alone, this desert prophet preached an unpopular sermon: Repent, reform, change your life! No one likes to be told what to do and no one likes the inference that he or she is not living a good life.

From the Sadducees and Pharisees, religious leaders of the day, John demanded evidence in action, not merely words, that they meant to reform before they could "step forward for this bath" of baptism. John was firm. He insisted that their privileged position and their claim that Abraham was their father could not be a substitute for true repentance and good deeds.

How alone John must have felt! He is the sign, like Elijah in the Old Testament, that God's return is at hand. Let us listen to his voice and find the courage to speak his message. May we not only *hear* his words of reform, but begin to *live* a life of repentance.

TALKING

1. Talk about the life of John the Baptist. Note the similarities to Elijah's life (Mal 3:1).
2. What could you do as a family to show your willingness to "step forward for this bath"?
3. Share your answers:
   I am afraid to speak before others when _____.
   To change my life I will _____.
   My response to the words and lifestyle of John the Baptist would have been
   _____.

DOING

1. Plan a celebration for Mary on December 8. Read her canticle in Luke 1:46-55. Notice the different ways Mary is depicted in your church (stained-glass windows, statues, stations of the cross, and so forth.)

2. Make your weekly scripture symbol—a megaphone with the words "Prepare the way." Place it in your home or on your SUNDAY THROUGHOUT THE YEAR banner.

PRAYING

(In preparation, light two candles of the Advent wreath and fill the cup of blessing. Then gather around the Advent wreath and offer the following prayer.)

Lord,
Help us to prepare for your coming by doing ordinary things in an extraordinary way. May we find the courage to be like John the Baptist, a voice in the desert, preparing the way for the Lord to come.

We drink from our blessing cup as a sign that we are one as a family as we prepare the way of the Lord.

(In silence, pass the cup around for each family member to drink.)

Dec 4, 1983 / Dec 7, 1986

3rd Sunday of Advent (Mt 11:2-11)

REFLECTING

Who am I? Where am I going? What is my relationship to others? What is my relationship to God?

We spend a lifetime seeking our identity. The discovery of our self and the affirmation of that self cannot be made alone, but only in relationship with others. We hold within ourselves a mystery, a mystery that is slowly revealed to us as we interact with God and with his people. We slowly become who we already are.

And in this slow process of discovering who we are, we have to know and affirm who Jesus is. We know Jesus through what he said and did. He is the gentle healer, the healer of the blind, the crippled, the sick, the deaf, the poor. He is the Good News. If John had been with Jesus, if he had heard his words and witnessed his actions, he would not have had to ask from prison: "Are you the one or should we look for another?"

From Jesus' response, we know that he did not see John's question as an indication of a lack of faith. On the contrary, Jesus praises John for his greatness, for his fidelity in preparing the way of the Lord, for his faith in proclaiming him as the long-awaited one.

We are called to have faith, the same faith as that of the apostles, of John, of all men and women before us who lived the Good News. And to discover who we are, we must be healed, healed in mind, healed of jealousy and self-hatred, healed of the hurt we have caused or received. As followers of Jesus, we are to bring this gift of healing to others. In this act, we discover who Jesus is and in so doing begin to discover who we are.

TALKING

1. Discuss the ways we discover ourselves and others. Have each family member respond to the question, "Who am I?"

2. Who is Jesus? How do you get to know him? Affirm your faith in him and through him affirm who you are.

3. Share your answers:
   The question I would like to ask Jesus is _____.
   I offer healing to others by _____.
   Right now in my personal growth I am _____.

DOING

1. Plan a ceremony centered around arranging your creche. Place photos or silhouettes of each family member in the nativity scene. Place Jesus and the star in the creche on Christmas Eve.

2. The scripture symbol for this week is the word "John." Place it in your home or on your SUNDAY THROUGHOUT THE YEAR banner.

PRAYING

(In preparation, light three candles of the Advent wreath and fill the cup of blessing. You will also need a bible. Gather around the Advent wreath and offer the following prayer.)

Lord,
You have shown us how to heal and be healed.
Let us be a sign of your healing power before others.

(In silence pass the cup around for each family member to drink.)

4th Sunday of Advent (Mt 1:18-24)

REFLECTING

Abraham and Sarah, Isaac and Rebecca, Jacob and Rachel, Moses, Ruth, David, Isaiah, Jeremiah. All these people held and lived the dream of the promised coming of the Messiah. And now, Mary.

In a dream, the messenger angel announced to Joseph the fulfillment of the promise of a Messiah:

> "The Virgin shall be with child
> and give birth to a son,
> and they shall call him Emmanuel."

The word "Emmanuel" means *God with us*. The presence of God is within all that we do. We welcome God into our lives when we recognize and celebrate his presence.

Through a young girl's trust in God, the promise of Jesus becomes a reality. His word takes on human life. Thinking about Mary brings us close to Christmas and the birth of her son, the promised Savior.

May we be filled with joy and thanksgiving as Jesus comes into our lives and we begin to live his life.

TALKING

1. Talk about Mary and her trust in God.

2. Joseph received Mary into his home. Discuss ways we welcome and receive people into our homes. How can we develop the art of hospitality?

3. Share your answers:
   My favorite Old Testament person, a person who dreamed the impossible dream made possible in Jesus, is _____.
   As a family we recognize "God with us" in _____.
   To keep a dream alive, I _____.

DOING

1. Write a prayer for the blessing of your Christmas tree.

2. As your weekly scripture symbol, make a fleur-de-lis, a sign for Mary. Place it in your home or on your SUNDAY THROUGHOUT THE YEAR banner.

PRAYING

(In preparation, light four candles of the Advent wreath and fill the blessing cup. Then gather around the Advent wreath and offer the following prayer.)

Lord,
We pray for families everywhere. May their hearts be filled with the joy of your coming. In your name, Emmanuel, may they know God with us. We thank you for Mary and rejoice in the trust and hope she lived. May we live your life as the promised one.

(Pray the Hail Mary together.)

We drink from our blessing cup as a sign that we are one as a family as we wait for Emmanuel.

(In silence, pass the cup around for each family member to drink.)

Feast of the Holy Family (Mt 2:13-15, 19-23)

REFLECTING

Our refrigerator door tells the weekly story of our family life. On it we list things to do, people who need our prayers, and events that we have celebrated or are preparing to celebrate. We record moments of thanksgiving and gratitude for different people in our life. Because we are a family, we try to share all the moments of our life: love, joy, sadness, loneliness, success and failure, work and play, prayer and thanksgiving.

In today's second reading (Col 3:12-21), Paul speaks of the environment necessary for the growth of each family member. When we imitate Christ, we free one another to be the person God calls each of us to be.

It is not easy to live as a family, to live in love, harmony and mutual respect. Genuine family life requires hard work and practice. The responsibilities of family living are mutual; they are shared by *all* the members of the family. Each of us is called to bring forth the best in the others. Indeed, the Spirit of Christ is present in each home because this same Spirit dwells within each family member.

Let us be profoundly thankful for one another and for the Spirit who makes family life possible.

TALKING

1. Talk about the environment necessary for family growth. Which virtues do you need to develop? Which of these virtues do you find hardest to live as a person? as a family? Which is the easiest?

2. Share your answers:
   I have this duty toward my family: _____.
   In my family living, I am most thankful for _____.
   For me, the Holy Family is _____.

DOING

1. Place lists with these headings on your refrigerator door: "Things to do," "We pray for," "We are thankful for," "We celebrate," "We are family." Under the last heading, place your family names. Fill in these lists during the next few weeks.

2. Make your weekly scripture symbol—the words "We are family." Place it in your home or on your SUNDAY THROUGHOUT THE YEAR banner.

PRAYING

Response: Thank you, God.

You call each of us to grow in a family as Jesus did with Mary and Joseph ...
You call us to live with a heart of compassion, to be patient, kind and humble ...
You call us to bear with one another, to forgive quarrels as soon as they begin.

Because of your love for us, Lord, you call us to live as your family. We are grateful for your presence within each of us. Help us to build up the spirit of one another. Help us to show our joy and appreciation for each member of our family.

(Family members say to one another: (*name*), thank you for being in our family. I love you.)

CYCLE A

Feast of the Baptism of the Lord (Mt 3:13-17)

REFLECTING

After a bombing, a statue of Christ was discovered with no arms. Across the bottom of the statue someone had written: I have no hand but yours.

Like Jesus, we are called to accept our ministry in doing the work of the Father. Jesus officially begins his work through his baptism. In today's gospel, Matthew shows Jesus anointed for his mission. Through our baptism we are commissioned to go forth in the Spirit and become Christ's hands in a hurting world.

Jesus did not need baptism as we do, but his baptism tells us that God is with him in a special way. As Jesus was baptized by John in the River Jordan, he received approval from his father. The Holy Spirit descended on him like a dove and the voice of the Father was heard: "This is my Son, the Beloved; my favor rests on him."

We, too, are in God's favor. Through our baptism we belong to the family of God. We call God our Father for we are his children, brothers and sisters to one another. It is through our baptism that we are called to work together as a family.

Through our baptism, may we remain turned toward God. Together may we share in the mission of Jesus, a mission of sharing with others the blessings we have received.

TALKING

1. Have family members tell about the work they do. Give each person a sign of approval and a vote of confidence in this work.

2. Talk about the baptism of each family member. Recall the people present. Recall the promises made. Familiarize yourself with the gestures and signs of baptism: lighted candle, white garment, water, words, profession of faith. Make plans to renew your baptism commissioning to do the work of the Lord.

3. Share your answers:
   Let your favor rest on me as I _____.
   For me, my baptism was _____.
   As Christ's hands, I will _____.

DOING

1. Have each member of the family trace an outline of his or her hand on a piece of paper. Write the person's name inside the hand. Place the cutout hands on a banner marked "I have no hands but yours."

2. Make your weekly scripture symbol—a sign of water. Place it in your home or on your SUNDAY THROUGHOUT THE YEAR banner.

PRAYING

God, our Father,
Through baptism, we are your children, your sons and daughters. Continue to show your approval of us. Commission us, anoint us, as you did your son Jesus, to go forth and share your blessings with others. You speak with us in all that we do. As we listen, please give us direction in the work we are doing and confidence to do that work. Amen.

(Bless each family member with water in the sign of the cross.)

2nd Sunday of Ordinary Time (Jn 1:29-34)

REFLECTING

Have you ever experienced wonder? Have you ever known joy? Have you ever been surprised by hope?

Many times these moments arrive unexpectedly in our lives. We welcome them in awe and discover through them a reality beyond the one we live daily. Some people see signs in these experiences, transcendent signs that tell us of God's presence.

John the Baptist confessed that at first he did not recognize Jesus. It was only when he saw the presence of the Spirit with Jesus that John exclaimed, "This is God's chosen one!" In that experience, in the sign of the Spirit, John recognized the one who baptizes with the Spirit.

In this experience John proclaimed a reality. He saw more than the man Jesus walking toward him.
> "Look! There is the Lamb of God
> who takes away the sin of the world!"

John the evangelist combines the lamb image with Isaiah's image of God's suffering servant who bears the sin of the world.

Like John, may we welcome the Spirit into our lives so that we are able to see in our ordinary experiences the presence of God and are able to respond with the psalmist, "Here I am, Lord; I come to do your will."

TALKING

1. Share an experience of hope, joy or wonder which came unexpectedly. How did you handle this experience?
2. The presence of the Spirit helps us to know Jesus. Talk about the New Testament stories in which Jesus was not immediately recognized (e.g., Jn 4:4-42 and Lk 24:13-35).
3. Share your answers:
   I find it hard for me to recognize Jesus when _____.
   Upon seeing Jesus I would have proclaimed _____.
   During the breaking of the bread at Mass, I say _____.

DOING

1. Relate an experience you've had with each of the following symbols: ring, heart, hand. What does each symbol mean for you? What is your symbol for each of the following?
   joy _____
   hope _____
   wonder _____

2. Make a lamb for your weekly scripture symbol. Place it in your home or on your SUNDAY THROUGHOUT THE YEAR banner.

PRAYING

Response: This is God's chosen one.
Jesus, you came walking to John and he exclaimed ...
You come into our lives to teach us how to love and we say ...
You come to show us how to forgive and we say ...
You come to share your life with us and we say ...

May we recognize you, Lord, in the life we live daily and know the presence of your Father in our experiences of hope, wonder and joy. Amen.

3rd Sunday of Ordinary Time (Mt 4:12-17)

REFLECTING

"Come on, follow me. I know the way," your friend shouts as you walk through the woods together. It is dark. You are afraid. You do not like following an unknown path. Yet this is what Jesus asked of his apostles and also asks of you.

Jesus goes to Galilee and becomes a guide to the people as Isaiah had foretold. He calls different people to follow him. To the fishermen, Simon, Andrew, James and John, he calls, "Come after me." They must have been afraid to begin a new way, to follow a new path of life.

Like the apostles, we are afraid when Jesus asks us to come after him and to see in him the light and hope of God's salvation. How quickly do we respond?

TALKING

1. Imagine a marvelous fishing day. Share the way you think the brothers must have felt leaving their fishing nets to follow Jesus. What might they have said to one another and to Jesus?

2. Have a contest naming as many Old and New Testament people as you can who responded to the call, "Come follow me."

3. Share your answers:
   My response to Jesus' invitation would have been _____.
   The people in my life who bring me hope and light are _____.
   I find it (hard/easy) to follow an unknown path because _____.

DOING

1. Invite grandparents or any elderly person in the community to come to your home for dinner or to come to Sunday Mass with you and your family.

2. This week's scripture symbol is a fish. Place the symbol you make in your home or on your SUNDAY THROUGHOUT THE YEAR banner.

PRAYING

Response: Come after me.
God, you said to Noah, Abraham, Isaac and Jacob . . .
You said to Moses, Joseph, kings and prophets . . .
Jesus, you said to Peter, Andrew, James and John . . .
You said to fishermen, teachers and workers . . .
You say to men, women, boys and girls, to (*say each family member's name*) . . .

Lord,
You said, "Come after me, and I will show you a new way to live." Give us the courage to follow and live this new life with you. As a family, we will help one another come after you. Amen.

4th Sunday of Ordinary Time (Mt 5:1-12a)

REFLECTING

All of us want to be happy. All of us ask the simple question that men and women have asked since the beginning of time: *How* can I be happy?

Jesus taught us a way to happiness. A way to live in his kingdom now and forever is to live the life of the beatitudes. The word "beatitude" means happiness, and each of the eight beatitudes presented by Matthew in Jesus' Sermon on the Mount defines for us a faith that is lived daily.

The beatitudes are given not as law but as gospel, the good news that tells us to rely on God as our strength and the foundation of our life.

As a family may we live together the blessings of the beatitudes.

TALKING

1. Read Isaiah 61:1-3. Discuss your declaration of happiness.

2. Beatitudes define a lived faith. How do you show others that God's kingdom has begun, that the reign of God's love is present among us?

3. Read the beatitudes and share your answers to the following:
   I was pleased to hear that _____.
   I was surprised to hear that _____.
   With the beatitudes I hope that _____.

DOING

1. The word "blessed" can be translated as "Congratulations." Restate the beatitudes in this light. Congratulate different members of your family for their living of the various beatitudes.

2. Make your weekly scripture symbol—two faces with "Congratulations" below. Place it in your home or on your SUNDAY THROUGHOUT THE YEAR banner.

PRAYING

(Have one family member read the following slowly and reflectively.)

The air is warm. The sky holds no clouds. You are sitting on dry grass at the bottom of a hill. The land stretches flat before the hill. People have gathered. All eyes are on one man. You listen as he speaks: (Read the beatitudes, Matthew 5:1-12).

CYCLE A

5th Sunday of Ordinary Time (Mt 5:13-16)

REFLECTING

In a small village in one of the islands off New Guinea, salt is made every six months. The salt maker is considered the most important person in the village. For these villagers, salt is the most needed of all commodities and the most expensive.

One of the images in today's gospel is that of salt. We know that if salt loses its quality then it is useless. Salt flavors and preserves food. Jesus calls us to become the salt of the earth. Just as salt enhances the taste of food and yet does not change the food itself, so we are asked to enhance the gifts of others, not change them, and to help others share and rejoice in their gifts. If we live the life of the beatitudes, we will be the salt that flavors the earth; we will be the savor that brings joy and hope to all people.

Jesus also uses light as a symbol in this gospel. All of us have experienced personally the meaning of light in our lives. When we have a blackout we realize how much a lighted lamp in our home means. Jesus is the light of the world; he calls each of us to let his light shine through us to others. He asks us not to be afraid, not to hide his light in us.

What a privilege to be called to become the salt of the earth and the light of the world. What an honor to continue the mission of Jesus in making this old world into a new one.

TALKING

1. Name the different ways salt is used.
   I can become "salt" to another by _____.
2. The image of salt is used in Wisdom literature.
   What is it to be wise? For me, wisdom is _____.
3. Jesus was referred to as the light of the world. He now calls us to be a light. What is the meaning of the paschal candle and the candles used at Mass?
   I can become a light to others by _____.

DOING

1. Place a candle in the center of the table and light it for all family meals this week.

2. Make your weekly scripture symbol—a lighted candle. Place it in your home or on your SUNDAY THROUGHOUT THE YEAR banner.

PRAYING

(Place a dish of salt on the table. Light the family candle as a sign of Christ, the light of the world. Each family member should be holding one candle.)

Response: We will let our light shine.
From New York, (*name of your state*), Florida, California, Minnesota, (one family member lights his or her candle) . . .
From our cities, villages, and towns, (light another candle) . . .
From our hope and love, our joy and giving, (light another candle) . . .

Lord,
(*Names of all family members*), promise to become your light to others. Help us never to be afraid to let that light shine. We pass and taste this salt as a sign that we are willing to flavor the earth with your love. Amen.

(Sing "This Little Light of Mine.")

Feb 5, 1984 / Feb 8, 1987

6th Sunday of Ordinary Time (Mt 5:17-37)

REFLECTING

> So then, if you are bringing your offering to the altar and there remember that your brother has something against you, leave your offering there before the altar, go and be reconciled with your brother first, and then come back and present your offering.
>
> *—Matthew 5:23*

How beautiful these words are and how well they express the life we are called to live in our families and in our communities! Our actions must show what is in our hearts. The outer, visible living of the law must reflect our inner intentions.

As the people of God we look forward to the accomplishment of everything promised and commanded in the law. Jesus is our guide. He came to do the will of God, to accomplish what the living of the law promised.

Scripture is fulfilled not only in the prophetic sense but in the ethical demands that can be found in the law. The life that Jesus lived was in sharp contrast to the life of the scribes and Pharisees who concentrated on the letter of the law, but sometimes missed the spirit of that law.

The commands set forth in today's gospel are radical not just because they are so demanding, but because they touch the heart of what it is to be human; they reach the root of our relationship with others. What we say and do must express what is in our hearts.

TALKING

1. As a family, evaluate the demands made by Jesus in today's gospel. What demand do you find easiest? Hardest? Based on the lifestyle of the 20th century, what new demands would you add?

2. Share your answers:
   I am tempted to concentrate on the letter of the law when _____.

   I try to handle my anger by _____.
   These demands of Jesus are _____.

DOING

1. Introduce the custom of family members gathering on Saturday night to prepare for Sunday Mass. At this gathering, ask one another's forgiveness for any hurts during the week.

2. Make your weekly scripture symbol—a tablet of the law. Hang it in your home or on your SUNDAY THROUGHOUT THE YEAR banner.

PRAYING

Lord,
Keep us faithful to your law. Let us see clearly what you ask of each of us in our life.
(Sit quietly. Read the opening scripture passage in Reflecting. Listen. Read it again. Talk with God about how you feel about this passage. Thank God for being in your life.)

Feb 12, 1984 / Feb 15, 1987

7th Sunday of Ordinary Time (Mt 5:38-48)

REFLECTING

In 1980 riots filled the streets of San Salvador. Archbishop Romero was shot as he delivered a sermon demanding human rights for his people. As he lay dying, his prayer was one of forgiveness for his enemies.

We have only to look through history to know the many people who, like Archbishop Romero, imitated the life and words of Jesus on the cross: "Father, forgive them." In today's gospel Jesus tells us clearly that we are not only to pray for our enemies but to offer greetings to them. How easy it is to love those who love us, how difficult to love those who persecute, ridicule and reject us.

Here is the heart of the Sermon on the Mount, here is the ultimate demand: Love. To love is to be daily faithful to God's will. To love is to imitate God's love. It is overwhelming to even consider that we are capable of loving others and loving them as God loves. But in the Old Testament, "Be holy for I the Lord your God am holy," and in the New Testament, "Be perfect as your heavenly Father is perfect," we are reassured.

To journey toward perfection is to be faithful to God's will and to love his people. It is to be slow to anger, to offer compassion, to be rich in mercy. It is to be a spontaneous giver, to walk an extra mile, to reach out to those who have turned their backs on us. To do these difficult and demanding things, to love as Jesus loves, is to become a sign that the kingdom of God has indeed broken into our world. Love and be that sign.

TALKING

1. Talk about the demands of today's gospel. Too difficult? Too easy? Talk about the demands of your school, work, family. Too difficult? Too easy?

2. Share with family members the way you try to handle your feelings of rejection and ridicule.

3. Share your answers:
    When someone demands my best, I _____.
    I find it hard to offer love to _____.
    It is (hard/easy) for me to forgive my enemies because _____.

DOING

1. To demand the best from all family members, have a goal-setting session:
    Set individual goals (e.g., give more time to others, read more.)
    Set family goals (e.g., make more time for your family, welcome more people into your home.)
    Share and discuss goals. Set priorities.
    Mark the achievement of each goal during the year with a celebration.

2. Make your weekly scripture symbol—a "Be perfect" sign. Place it in your home or on your SUNDAY THROUGHOUT THE YEAR banner.

PRAYING

(With hands extended, offer this blessing to one another.)

May our lives be signs of the new life of the kingdom of God.
May our hearts welcome those who ridicule and reject us.
May we know that God's love rains on the just and the unjust.
May we grow in holiness and as a family become perfect as our heavenly Father is perfect. Amen.

8th Sunday of Ordinary Time (Mt 6:24-34)

REFLECTING

The fact that God loves us and constantly cares for us is so overwhelming that we are unable to live daily in recognition and acceptance of that love. Sometimes we act like lost people, frantically searching and anxiously worrying over our situation in life, so concerned about money, food and clothes.

How comforting are the words of today's gospel: We are cared for by God. We are only to look at the care God gives the wild flowers, which bloom brilliantly and live for only a short time, to be assured that God provides much more for each of us. And we are only to remember the beautiful and consoling God through the words of Isaiah: "I will never forget you."

This providing and caring, this remembering and loving God, asks us simply to set our priorities in life and to set them now. Our top priority must be to seek first the kingdom of God and to be single-minded in this seeking. Worry and anxiety only distract us from God. If our mind is set on God, then we will be able to gain the proper perspective toward worldly cares.

In our Eucharist celebrations the priest leads us in prayer: "Protect us from all anxiety as we wait in joyful hope for the coming of Jesus." As a family, let us help one another live lives of joy and hope. Let us ask ourselves: Where do we spend our time and energy? What are the values that help determine our choices? How can we free one another from the crippling force of worry? Let us have enough of worrying about tomorrow and "Let tomorrow take care of itself."

TALKING

1. Talk about the things that worry you most. Consider ways to handle this worry.
2. How can we remember God's love and our call to place him first in our lives?
3. Share your answers:
   When I become anxious, I _____.
   Knowing God loves and cares for me helps me to _____.
   The thing I worry about most in my life is _____.

DOING

1. You have $500 to spend. Make a list of what you would buy. Share the reasons for your choices with your family.
2. Make your weekly scripture symbol—a flower. Place it in your home or on your SUNDAY THROUGHOUT THE YEAR banner.

PRAYING

Become quiet.
Sit still in God's love. Feel the warmth of
   his love. Know that he made you and loves you.
Hear him speak: "I will never forget you."
Feel the comfort of these words.
Thank him for loving you.
Tell him of your love for him.

9th Sunday of Ordinary Time (Mt 7:21-27)

REFLECTING

In today's gospel Jesus states clearly that we must *practice* what we hear; we must put into action the word which Jesus has preached. To make sure we have no excuse for not understanding this message, Jesus gave us an example. In this example we have a choice. We can choose to be like a wise man who built his house on rock. This man had listened. He had heard what wind and rain can do to a house that does not have a firm foundation.

Or we can choose to be like the foolish man who also listened but did not put into practice what he had heard. He built his house on sandy soil and the wind and rain came and all was destroyed.

The choice is ours:
Listen and do. Take what you hear and put it into action. Your faith becomes stronger. You become an integrated human being. And when crises in your life come, your roots will be deep and strong, and you will be able to handle your problems. This is the way to life.
Or:
Listen only. When hardships come, you will be tossed at the mercy of the world; you will have nothing that gives you strength or offers you fortitude. This is the way to death.

Let us choose to live like Jesus, the man of action, who practiced what he preached. Let us build our house on rock.

TALKING

1. Choose and talk about an activity in your life that comes from your faith.

2. Recall a difficulty in your life. Reflect on the way you handled it. What or who was the source of affirmation?

3. Share your answers:
    The best way to overcome lethargy is to _____.
    To put into action what I hear, I _____.
    I have built my house on _____.

DOING

1. Write a family creed. Next to each statement write or draw what you do to live that belief. Place your creed on the kitchen floor.

2. Make your weekly scripture symbol—a house. Place it in your home or on your SUNDAY THROUGHOUT THE YEAR banner.

PRAYING

Lord, be my rock of safety. Be my rock of refuge, a stronghold to give me safety. You are my rock and my fortress;
   for your name's sake you will lead and guide me.
Lord, be my rock of safety.

—from the Responsorial Psalm of today's Mass

1st Sunday of Lent (Mt 4:1-11)

REFLECTING

"Lent is such a gloomy time."

"I always feel guilty for not doing enough."

"Six weeks, 40 days ... that's a long time."

Lent can be lived with a spirit of enthusiasm as we get ready for new life. Not only is Lent a good time to learn more about ourselves through penitential practices, but our prayer should be that we also become more docile to the promptings of the Spirit in our life.

At his baptism, Jesus was anointed with the Spirit for his mission. The spirit was with Jesus as he resisted the three temptations of the devil and chose to walk the road to Jerusalem, not as a great king, but as the suffering Son of God.

If we are trying to be true to our baptism, to our faith, we will not escape the same treatment that Jesus received. We, too, will be tried. And so during Lent we prepare ourselves by becoming more aware of our strengths and weaknesses. We prepare through what we do for others, through the way we talk and listen, in the way we think. We could choose self-denial, "giving up" something, fasting, or spending a certain time in prayer every day.

Let us prepare for our new life through Jesus as we allow ourselves to be led by the Spirit into the desert to pray.

TALKING

1. What is Lent? Is there a need for a Lenten time in our personal life and our family life?

2. Our goal during Lent is to learn to love more and to begin to use our gifts more.

3. Share your answers:
When I think of Jesus in the desert, I _____.
To prepare for Easter, I will _____.

DOING

1. Put a pretzel beside each plate at dinner. The folded pretzel reminds us of arms crossed in prayer. Save the pretzels until your family prayer (see below).

2. Make your weekly scripture symbol—a desert. Place it in your home or on your SUNDAY THROUGHOUT THE YEAR banner.

PRAYING

God,
Help us to find the way to follow your Son. Give us direction to choose those actions which bring us closer in knowing and loving you. May we begin to leave behind all things which prevent us from having you in our life. May we help one another prepare together during this Lent for new life. Amen.
(All eat pretzels together.)

CYCLE A

2nd Sunday of Lent (Mt 17:1-9)

REFLECTING

"Amazing!" "Incredible!" How often do we say or hear these words? When do we experience a sense of wonder in our lives?

In many gospel stories we read that the people marveled at what Jesus said and did. Have we lost the ability to marvel not only at what Jesus does now through others, but even at the wonder of God's creation?

Peter, James and John were awestruck as Jesus was transfigured before their eyes and his clothes became dazzling white. How else could they respond? Through this wonder-event they were given a glimpse into eternity, a hint of the life to come.

A wonder-experience renews and enlightens us. For one moment we see and understand. Like the three friends, let us fall face downward in the presence of God's love and in awe hear his voice: "This is my Son. Listen to him."

TALKING

1. Have all the family members describe what they see, hear, smell and feel when this gospel story is read. Children often have a graphic way of visualizing the gospel stories so they become more living for us.

2. Talk about one wonder-experience you have had—an experience of a sunset, the first spring flower, a newborn baby, etc.)

3. Renew family and individual Lenten resolutions.

4. Share your answers:
   I marvel at what Jesus did when he _____.
   For me, wonder is _____.
   I am in awe when _____.

DOING

1. In imitation of Jesus who revealed himself to his friends, have each family member say one good thing about himself or herself at supper.

2. Make your weekly scripture symbol—a cloud. Place it in your home or on your SUNDAY THROUGHOUT THE YEAR banner.

PRAYING

Response: We are overcome with awe.
Lord, you speak through all the creation which you have made . . .
You speak through the people that we see and meet daily . . .
You tell us who you are through the way you have lived and the way you ask
  us to live . . .
You tell us you are the Son of God and, like your three friends, we are astonished . . .

Lord,
Help us to have wonder in our lives. Help us to look at everything as if we were seeing it for the first time. You are wonder-filled! Amen.

3rd Sunday of Lent (Jn 4:5-42)

REFLECTING

What is your name? Where do you come from? What do you like to do? These are some of the questions we ask someone who is new in our neighborhood.

When Jesus arrived thirsty at a well in Samaria, a woman offered him a drink and began questioning him to discover who he was. It is interesting to note how slowly Jesus revealed himself to her.

First, the woman discovered that he was a Jewish holy man and was astonished that such a person would even speak with her. Jesus then exclaimed that the water he gives is different from the well water which never completely quenches your thirst. When Jesus revealed that he knew about her background and her five husbands, she marveled and called him a prophet.

They continued speaking together. The woman stated, "I know that Messiah—that is, Christ—is coming." Jesus replied, "I who am speaking to you, I am he." Jesus had revealed himself as a Jewish holy man and a prophet. Now he reveals himself as Messiah and Savior.

The woman had been persistent in her questioning, humble in her acceptance of herself. Now she becomes active in her new knowledge. She leaves and begins to tell others about Jesus. This woman's faith must be our faith. As men and women of faith, as families of faith, we must not only be questioning and searching for Jesus, but we must also be patient as he reveals himself. Then, in faith, we must bring others to him.

TALKING

1. Pretend you are a Samaritan. Would you have believed this woman when she told you about Jesus?

2. Why do you think Jesus revealed himself slowly?

3. Do you avoid the truth about yourself? How? Did this woman accept or avoid the truth about herself?

4. Share your answers:
   At the well, I would ask Jesus this question: _____.
   In a strange and new place, I feel _____.
   Right now, I feel I know Jesus as _____.

DOING

1. Make a collage of different pictures of water. List each of the sacraments on the collage. It is through the sacraments that we receive the living water as a gift of the Spirit. Place the words "Come and drink" across the top.

2. Make a well as your weekly scripture symbol. Place it in your home or on your SUNDAY THROUGHOUT THE YEAR banner.

PRAYING

Response: Lord, give me living water that I may never thirst again.
For the faith to hear your word with an open heart ...
For the courage to tell your word to others ...
For the patience to open our eyes to see you ...
For the love to accept the truth about ourselves ...

Lord,
Come into our life, and slowly show us who you are as you did this woman at the well. Help us to always search for you and to see and know your presence in all that we do. Amen.

Mar 25, 1984 / Mar 22, 1987

4th Sunday of Lent (Jn 9:1-41)

REFLECTING

Each of us has a faith story to tell. Our story began long ago when God called us to be his people. A personal version of our faith story begins with our baptism; it begins when we say, "Lord, I believe," and it unfolds as we are willing to stand for that belief.

In today's gospel we listen to the story of a blind man. Jesus healed the physical blindness for which the man was not responsible and then challenged some religious leaders to face the spiritual blindness for which they were responsible.

What a beautiful and simple story of a blind man's growth in seeing! The authorities challenged and ridiculed him, tried to dismiss his cure, tried to discredit Jesus who made the cure. The man was threatened with expulsion from the temple. To all of this, the man replied, "I was blind and now I can see." To Jesus, the man proclaimed, "Lord, I believe." As he stood up for Jesus, so his faith and his seeing increased.

Some of those who say they see grow increasingly blind, and those who are blind come to see. There is a difference in knowing and talking *about* God as these religious leaders did, and in coming into a personal faith relationship with him as did the blind man.

May we continue to grow in our belief and stand before others in faith as our story is lived.

TALKING

1. Lent began as a preparation for candidates for baptism. How does our baptism help us to see life in a different way?

2. Discuss the difference between knowing God and knowing about God. Discover one way the family members could live a life of seeing, of belonging to God, of acclaiming his presence in their lives this week.

3. We do not say disease is a result of sin or that some people deserve their misfortune. Talk about attitudes toward the handicapped and the unfortunate. What does Jesus say?

4. Share your answers:
   I am most blind when _____.
   In knowing about God, I _____.
   In knowing God, I _____.

DOING

1. Light a rose-colored candle (the color symbolizes encouragement) during the supper meals this week as a sign that we have the gift of faith from Jesus.

2. Make your weekly scripture symbol—a face with the words "I can see." Place it in your home or on your SUNDAY THROUGHOUT THE YEAR banner.

PRAYING

(With family members, renew your faith promise made at baptism.)

Response: We do.
Do you believe in God, the Father almighty, creator of heaven and earth?
Do you believe in Jesus Christ, his only Son, who was born of the virgin, was crucified, died and was buried, rose from the dead, and is now seated at the right hand of the Father?
Do you believe in the Holy Spirit, the holy Catholic church, the communion of saints, the forgiveness of sins, the resurrection of the body and life everlasting?
This is our faith. This is the faith of the church. We are proud to profess it, in Christ Jesus our Lord. Amen.

Apr 1, 1984 / Mar 29, 1987

5th Sunday of Lent (Jn 11:1-45)

REFLECTING

"Last week my grandmother died. I cried. She was a good friend of mine. I will miss her even though I know she is happy with God." A young student told this to his teacher.

Jesus experiences the same deep emotion at the death of his friend Lazarus. He weeps just as this young boy. How beautiful is this expression of the humanity of Jesus and how imitative we should be of his love and consolation for Martha and Mary.

After being informed of Lazarus' death, Jesus waits four days before going to Bethany. It was Jewish tradition that the soul stayed near the body for three days after death, and Jesus wants to make certain that Lazarus is dead. Martha knows him to be a healer bringing life to others, but now she will know him as Life. "I am the Life," Jesus says, the life that will never end. "Whoever lives and believes in me will never die."

Miracles are signs of God's glory. In this miracle, which parallels so closely his own death, Jesus helps the people in their belief by showing that he is life. He calls upon the Father and thanks him for having heard him. Jesus shows us that he does nothing on his own; only through the Father does he raise Lazarus from the dead. He calls us to have life, the fullness of life, a life that will go on forever, his life.

TALKING

1. Talk about the humanity of Jesus and the expression of deep love he felt for his friend Lazarus. Why are we sometimes afraid to express our feelings?
2. Share your answers:
   The words of consolation I would offer are _____.
   For me the humanity of Jesus shines forth when _____.
   Life is _____; living forever is _____.

DOING

1. Make hot cross buns. Place the cross in the center to show that even in death there is life and the glory of God.
2. Your weekly scripture symbol is the word "Life." Place it in your home or on your SUNDAY THROUGHOUT THE YEAR banner.

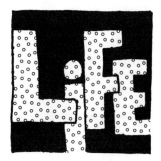

PRAYING

Dear God,
Help us to travel with Jesus not only in bringing life to others but also in walking the road of the cross. We know we are like Jesus when we weep for others, when we offer love and consolation. Help us, Lord, to live our lives fully alive to your will. Amen.

Passion Sunday (Mt 27:11-54, shorter)

REFLECTING

Though he was sinless, he suffered willingly for sinners.
Though innocent, he accepted death to save the guilty.
By his dying he has destroyed our sins.
By his rising he has raised us up
to holiness of life.

—from the Preface for Passion Sunday

When Jesus was accused by the chief priests and the elders, he did not answer them. When Pilate asked in amazement if he had not heard what they were saying about him, Jesus kept silent.

It is so easy to defend ourselves. We want others to know that we are right, that we have been misjudged. It is much harder to let our actions speak for us. But that is what Jesus chose to do. By his life he tells us who he is; by his death he speaks even more clearly. The question that Pilate asked him, "Are you the king of the Jews?" was answered by the Roman centurion who cried out at Jesus' death, "In truth this was a son of God."

May our actions speak clearly for us too. May they say that we too are sons and daughters of God, our Father.

TALKING

1. How do you feel when you are accused of something you have not done? How do your feelings differ if it is something you are guilty of?

2. Talk about one thing that Jesus' life says to you.

3. Share your answers:
   During this Holy Week I will let my action speak for me by
   _____.

   I am like the Roman centurion when I _____.

DOING

1. As a family, participate in the Holy Week activities in your parish.

2. Make your weekly scripture symbol—a cross. Place it in your home or on your SUNDAY THROUGHOUT THE YEAR banner.

PRAYING

Lord,
Help us to live so that our actions speak of our lives as children of God. Give us the strength to walk with you to Calvary and the faith to walk through death into eternal life with you. Amen.

2nd Sunday of Easter (Jn 20:19-31)

REFLECTING

"Two big days for churchgoers, Christmas and Easter. But I think the second is the most important. Christmas is the promise, but Easter is the proof," says Hip Shot in the comic strip, *Rick O'Shay*.

How hard it is sometimes to believe. How often each of us has asked for proof. Thomas represents all of us in his desire to *see* and to *touch* the risen Lord. Jesus tells us, "Happy are those who have not seen and yet believe."

In today's gospel John tells us that he recorded these signs to help us believe. It was through faith that the Christian community was formed as one people of God, loving and serving one another through the risen Lord. It is through faith that we grow as his people today.

TALKING

1. Place yourself in the upper room. How do you feel? What do you see? Use all your senses. Where are you standing? Would you be like Thomas or like another apostle in the room?

2. Name some signs of Christ in the world today that help you believe.

3. Share your answers:
   It is (easy/hard) to believe today because _____.

DOING

1. Pray alone at night, thanking God for the joy and peace that is now possible through faith in the risen Lord.

2. Make your weekly scripture symbol—a dove with an olive branch for peace. Place it in your home or on your SUNDAY THROUGHOUT THE YEAR banner.

PRAYING

Response: Give thanks to the Lord for he is good (Ps 118:2).
Joy is being aware of our inner being, our deep inside . . .
Joy is our deep inside *delighted* in seeing the goodness of others . . .
Joy is our deep inside *glad* to be aware of what life is . . .
Joy is our deep inside *rejoicing* in the meaning of creation . . .

Just as joy comes from the risen Lord, so does peace, the peace that only Jesus can give. In thanksgiving, let us now offer a sign of peace and joy to one another.
(Offer one another a sign of peace.)

CYCLE A

3rd Sunday of Easter (Lk 24:13-35)

REFLECTING

"Can you imagine!" "I don't know what to say." "It's hard to believe." Just as we talk excitedly about different events that have happened to us, so the disciples had a "lively exchange" as they walked to a village named Emmaus.

They did not recognize Jesus as he joined them on the road and asked them the cause for their discussion. These two men reveal to us what the community believed about Jesus: "a prophet powerful in word and deed." They also tell us of the hope they had that "he was the one to set Israel free." But now Jesus was dead and buried and the news reported that his body was not to be found in the tomb. These men were despondent.

As they continued walking, Jesus helped interpret the scripture about himself. When they arrived in Emmaus, the men asked him to stay with them. As they ate a meal together, Jesus broke the bread and began to distribute it to them. Only in the breaking of the bread did they recognize Jesus and only then did they take the time to remember how their hearts were burning inside when they heard him explain the scripture to them.

TALKING

1. Are we slow to believe? If so, why?

2. Jesus was recognized in the stranger who had walked with them. How do we grow to see Jesus in the strangers in our own lives? Read Matthew 25:37-40.

3. Share your answers:
   In the "breaking of the bread," I _____.
   I recognize Jesus in _____.

DOING

1. Role play this gospel story or another scripture story in which Jesus shares a meal.

2. Make your weekly scripture symbol—a loaf of bread with the word "Emmaus" on it. Place it in your home or on your SUNDAY THROUGHOUT THE YEAR banner.

EMMAUS

PRAYING

Response: Lord, help us to grow in knowing you.
Through our baptism and confirmation . . .
Through our prayers . . .
Through your teachings . . .
Through the stranger . . .
Through our celebration of the Eucharist and your presence in the breaking of the bread . . .
Through forgiving and being forgiven in the sacrament of reconciliation . . .

Lord Jesus,
Make your word plain to us. Make our hearts burn with love when you speak. Amen.

(As a family choose and sing a gospel acclamation.)

4th Sunday of Easter (Jn 10:1-10)

REFLECTING

"I think everyone is here. Let's see "Freddie? Maura? James? Ethel? We're all ready, let's go."

We need someone in our life to give us direction, to call us together, to help us stay together. We need a leader. It is good when that leader is also our friend.

Jesus is our leader and friend. He calls himself the Good Shepherd. We are his sheep. If we listen, we will hear him call us by name. As his sheep, we will know and follow only his voice. Not only does a shepherd know all his sheep, but being a good shepherd he lays down his life for those in his care. King David was a shepherd who once protected his flock at the risk of his own life. Jesus becomes our Good Shepherd when he lays downs his life for us, his sheep.

Jesus also calls himself the sheepgate. In open country, the shepherd would sleep across the corral opening and have his body become the protecting door. We are welcome to come through this gate, through Jesus, to receive life, life in all its fullness.

TALKING

1. Name all the qualities that you think a shepherd should have. Name stories in which Jesus shows the qualities of a good shepherd. Read the story of young David as a shepherd in the Old Testament, 1 Samuel 16:1-13. Talk about other shepherd stories that you know.

2. Discuss the different "voices" of our culture that call on us. How do you listen and know the voice of Jesus?

3. Share your answers:
   As the Good Shepherd, Jesus _____.
   As a family we experience "life in all its fullness" when we _____.

   As a sheep, I follow Jesus by _____.

DOING

1. Write a secret note to a member of your family telling him or her why you are happy that all of you belong to the same Good Shepherd. (Choose names secretly so that every family member will receive a message.)

2. Make your weekly scripture symbol—a shepherd's crook. Place it in your home or on your SUNDAY THROUGHOUT THE YEAR banner.

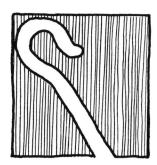

PRAYING

Jesus, our Good Shepherd,
Give direction to our lives. Help us to see the good, to find the true, and to enjoy the beautiful. Protect us from fear. Please guide us to know your will in all that we do. Amen.

5th Sunday of Easter (Jn 14:1-12)

REFLECTING

> Two roads diverged in a wood, and I—
> I took the one less traveled by,
> And that has made all the difference.

—Robert Frost
The Road Not Taken

In a warm conversation during the Last Supper, Thomas and the other disciples were stunned into silence when Jesus announced he must leave them. Thomas asked for direction on how to get where Jesus was going. Tenderly, Jesus answered, "I am the Way, the Truth and the Life." Like Thomas, if we follow and do what Jesus has done, we too will have truth and life; we will be at home with him and the Father.

The road we choose to take must be one of faith. To travel the faith road, we must live turned to God, dependent upon him for all that we do. Jesus has said that if we have faith in him, we have faith in the Father, for he and the Father are one. Jesus has promised us that with faith we will be able to do his works. The works of the Father through Jesus were to teach, heal and comfort. They were the works of helping to discover truth, life and love. When we do these works, we can say with Jesus, "It is the Father who lives in me accomplishing his works."

The road of faith is a road not traveled by everyone in the 20th century. But the choice to follow this road *will make all the difference.*

TALKING

1. Choose and talk about the most difficult choice you have had to make in your life. How did you make it? What people helped you in this decision?

2. In this Last Supper discussion, Jesus assures the apostles that he will come back. When we say "Come, Lord" (*Maranatha*) we could mean not just the final coming but his daily coming into our life. Talk about the ways we can welcome this coming.

3. Share your answers:
   For me, the road of faith is easy/hard because _____.
   When I choose to help someone that no one likes, I feel _____.
   When I make a decision that is different from that of my group of friends (the road less traveled), I feel _____.

DOING

1. You have only a knapsack for a journey. List the things you would choose to take for your journey of faith.

2. Make your weekly scripture symbol—a winding road. Place it in your home or on your SUNDAY THROUGHOUT THE YEAR banner.

PRAYING

Response: We choose to follow Jesus as the way, the truth, and the life.
When we leave behind our selfishness ...
When we overcome our fear ...
When we welcome the coming of Jesus daily in our life ...
When we take the risk to love and trust others ...

Help us, Jesus, to have faith in you and to do the works that you do. Help us to say with you, "It is the Father who lives in me accomplishing his works." Amen.

May 20, 1984 / May 17, 1987

6th Sunday of Easter (Jn 14:15-21)

REFLECTING

"Goodbye. Have a good trip. We'll miss you. It's really sad to see you go. So long." People leave for college, vacation, travel, or move to another town. There is always the fear and sadness that we will never see them again.

Jesus prepared the apostles for his leaving (Ascension Thursday) by telling them that they would never be left alone like orphans, but that the Spirit of Truth would come (Pentecost). It is this Spirit that helped them to know the presence of Jesus in their lives even when they were no longer able to see him with their eyes. However, the people of the world who did not believe would see him no longer.

Jesus asked the apostles to love him and to follow his commandments, for this is the way to have life. This is the way to experience the love of the Father. There is only *one* commandment, the single command to love. If we love Jesus, then we have love for one another. When we live the values and commands Jesus lived in his own life— humility, joy, peace, doing the will of the Father—we are living his commandments.

It is also the Spirit of Truth that helps us to understand the presence of the Father, Son and Holy Spirit in our lives. Pentecost brings the Spirit and our confirmation seals us in that Spirit.

With the Spirit in our lives, we will never be orphans. How comforting is this lived promise!

TALKING

1. Talk about confirmation. Have each family member recall his or her own personal experience of this sacrament.
2. Share your answers:
   Today Jesus continues to reveal himself to us by _____.
   The value Jesus lived that I find most attractive is _____.
   The promise of the Spirit fills me with _____.

DOING

1. On a poster, make a list of the different commands that flow from the one single command to love.
2. Make your weekly scripture symbol—a heart with a commandment table inside. Place it in your home or on your SUNDAY THROUGHOUT THE YEAR banner.

PRAYING

(As a sign of the Spirit at our side, stand around the supper table and place your hand on the shoulder of the person next to you. Offer a word of encouragement and support in living the life of the Spirit.)

Dear Holy Spirit,
With your presence, we are not orphans. Continue to enlighten us, protect us, direct us and govern us always. Amen.

7th Sunday of Easter (Jn 17:1-11a)

REFLECTING

When can one pray? *Where* can one pray? *How* can one pray? *Why* should one pray? In our daily living, how does one find time to talk with God and listen to him?

Jesus was a praying man. He prayed before any decision, before teaching, before healing. He prayed out of the situation in which he was living, out of the fears, hopes and dreams of his daily life. Not only did he pray for his friends, the disciples, in their mission of forming a church, and for all future believers, but he showed the effect of that prayer by giving his life.

In today's gospel John shows us Jesus praying for unity, asking that we be in the Father and him as he and the Father are in each other. We are told that the only way the world will believe is to see our oneness. What an enormous responsibility!

TALKING

1. "When you pray, go to your room and close the door." Could you carry your room inside of you? Where do you find the best place to pray?
2. In what situations do you find the most need to talk with God?
3. Jesus showed forth the glory of God. How can we show this glory?
4. Share your answers:
   When I am happy, I pray _____.
   When everything goes wrong, I pray _____.
   When I am going to do something that is hard, I pray _____.

DOING

1. Make a clock. Have each family member sign his or her name for a particular time and place for prayers that day.
2. Make your weekly scripture symbol—a sign of hands in prayer. Place it in your home or on your SUNDAY THROUGHOUT THE YEAR banner.

PRAYING

Lord,
Teach us to pray. Teach us to talk with your Father as you talked with him. Teach us to listen. Help us to know your presence wherever we are and in whatever we are doing. Help us to pray alone and with others. Lord, teach us to pray. Amen.

(Hold hands and say the Our Father as a sign of the oneness of the family of God.)

Trinity Sunday (Jn 3:16-18)

REFLECTING

How do we welcome visitors to our home? What do we say? What do we do? How do we welcome visitors to our church?

In the second reading (2 Cor 13:11-13) Paul tells the Corinthians to greet one another with the kiss of peace, the same sign we offer to one another in the Mass. And Paul offers the following prayer: "The grace of the Lord Jesus Christ, the love of God and the fellowship of the Holy Spirit be with you all." Paul calls upon the Trinity in his plea for unity between the arguing Corinthians and the apostles. In this he reflects the prayer of Jesus that all may be one as he and the Father and the Spirit are one.

May we always welcome visitors to our home and to our church in a spirit of peace and good will. May the peace of the Lord be with all of us.

Help us to live the life of unity lived most fully in the Trinity, Father, Son and Holy Spirit.

TALKING

1. Talk about ways you handle and solve arguments as a family. Consider ways to eliminate "winners" and "losers." How do you find the courage to ask for or offer forgiveness?

2. In what ways are you able to show unity as a family? Consider different greetings and ways of welcoming others that would help to make them feel at home in your family.

3. Share your answers:
   I believe in the Father who _____.
   I believe in the Son who _____.
   I believe in the Holy Spirit who _____.

DOING

1. Make a mobile of circles. On each circle, write one belief from the Apostles' Creed. Display the mobile in your home.

2. Make your weekly scripture symbol—a trefoil. Place it in your home or on your SUNDAY THROUGHOUT THE YEAR banner.

PRAYING

Blessed Holy Trinity,
May we praise and honor you always by saying:
> Glory be to the Father, and to the Son, and to the Holy Spirit. As it was in the beginning, is now and ever shall be, world without end. Amen

(Offer one another a kiss of peace.)

Solemnity of Corpus Christi (Jn 6:51-59)

REFLECTING

One bread, one body, one Lord of all,
One cup of blessing which we bless
And we though many, throughout the earth,
We are one body in this one Lord.

—John Foley, S.J.,
One Bread, One Body

The melody which accompanies these beautiful lyrics lingers with us. These words reflect the life and spirit of our second reading (1 Cor 10:16-17).

The body and blood of Christ make us one. Though many, we become one body just as the many grains of wheat become one bread. To share in the one Lord is to share with one another. We are united as a community.

Paul's mention of the cup of blessing reminds us of the cup of wine that was shared to end a meal. With this cup, a blessing of thanksgiving to God was offered. The gesture of lifting the cup, passing it and tasting the wine showed gratitude to God and to his people gathered at the meal. In this Jewish custom, these words were spoken: "Blessed are you, Lord, God of all creation, creator of the fruit of the vine." These words are reminiscent of the words we pray in the meal of the Eucharist.

On this feast of Corpus Christi (Body of Christ) we celebrate the gift of Jesus himself in the meal of the Eucharist. In receiving the Eucharist, we become united with Jesus and with one another as an everlasting gift to the Father.

Let us celebrate our oneness in Christ through the bread we eat and the wine we drink, his body and blood, at our Eucharist meal. As his people, let us grow in oneness.

TALKING

1. Talk about what unites you as a family and as a community. What divides each of these groups?

2. As a family, reflect on your participation, celebration and reception of the Eucharist.

3. Share your answers:
   My blessing for my family is _____.
   In thanksgiving, I say _____.
   For me, Corpus Christi is _____.

DOING

1. Decorate a window in your home with paper cutouts of a loaf of bread, a cup of wine, the names of each family member, and the words "We are one." Write and say a blessing for your home.

2. Make your weekly scripture symbol—a loaf of bread and a cup of wine. Place it in your home or on your SUNDAY THROUGHOUT THE YEAR banner.

PRAYING

(Fill a blessing cup. Close your family meal with the following prayer.)

Lord,
We hold this cup and ask for your blessing. We give thanks and praise for the gift of yourself in the meal of the Eucharist. Though many, we are made one in your life. You are our one bread, our one body, our one Lord of all in this one world. Thank you.

(In silence pass the blessing cup for each family member to drink.)

13th Sunday of Ordinary Time (Mt 10:37-42)

REFLECTING

In many cultures, it is the custom to have open house on New Year's Day. People gather and wish one another hope and joy for the coming year. What a wonderful sign of hospitality!

There are many stories in the Old and New Testaments of people welcoming others into their homes. In our first reading, the generous and wealthy woman of Shunem offers food and a room to the prophet Elisha and his companion. Jesus was a guest in many different homes. Paul's travels were made possible by the hospitality of many people.

We should try to create welcoming environments in our homes and churches. The art of hospitality is to put people at ease, to allow them to feel comfortable and at home in new surroundings. Friendship can be offered and accepted only in an atmosphere of hospitality.

In today's gospel Jesus says, "Anyone who welcomes you welcomes me; and those who welcome me welcome the one who sent me."

It is in our family that we develop an attitude of welcome, that we practice hospitality. May the welcome mat at our door be a sign that our house is open to those who continue the mission of Jesus.

TALKING

1. Recall experiences or events where you felt comfortable and welcome. What contributed to this feeling of hospitality?

2. Talk about the different people of the Old Testament and the New Testament who welcomed guests into their homes. List the homes where Jesus stayed.

3. Share your answers:
   I can show hospitality by _____.
   To place God first in my life, I _____.
   One way to put people at ease is _____.

DOING

1. Invite a family to your home for Sunday dinner.

2. Make your weekly scripture symbol—a mat with "Welcome" on it. Place it in your home or on your SUNDAY THROUGHOUT THE YEAR banner.

PRAYING

Response: We welcome you, Jesus, into our life.
When we welcome the stranger and people we do not like ...
When we welcome the lowly ones ...
When we offer a friendly greeting ...
When we open our doors to the lonely, the forgotten, the rejected ...

Lord,
Help us as a family to live a life of hospitality toward your people. May our homes welcome you always.

14th Sunday of Ordinary Time (Mt 11:25-30)

REFLECTING

> "Come to me, all you who are weary and find life burdensome, and I will refresh you."
>
> *— Matthew 11:28, NAB*

These poetic words have been put to music by the Monks of the Weston Priory on their album, *Locusts and Wild Honey*. The music captures the spirit of this gospel message. The message brings comfort and solace to our life. Life does have burdens; we do become weary. But we are told to take heart, for Jesus will refresh us.

To be renewed in our daily living, we imitate the way Jesus lived his life: "Learn of me for I am meek and humble of heart."

In today's gospel, Jesus prays the *berakah*, a prayer of praise. We pray this same form of prayer during the Liturgy of the Eucharist. In the *berakah* prayer form we remember, we compliment and we hope. Divided into three parts, a *berakah* begins with an invitation to praise. The second part praises God, remembers and compliments him for all that he has done. The third part asks God to continue his loving actions today and all days as he has done in the past. Like Jesus, let us begin to pray the *berakah* in our own life.

TALKING

1. Discuss ways for a family to take up the yoke of Jesus and make light the burdens of life.
2. How can we imitate the gentleness and meekness of Jesus?
3. Share your answers:
   I am weary when _____.
   When life is burdensome, I _____.
   For me, rest and peace is _____.

DOING

1. Write and pray a *berakah*. Compliment God daily in your life.
2. Make your weekly scripture symbol—a yoke. Place it in your home or on your SUNDAY THROUGHOUT THE YEAR banner.

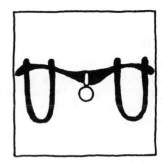

PRAYING

Response: We praise you. We bless you. We thank you.
God, for calling us to continue your works ...
God, for revealing yourself through your Son, Jesus ...
God, for helping us to find rest and peace ...

God,
We go to your Son and take his yoke upon our shoulders. Help us to learn from him, for he is gentle and humble of heart. Amen.

15th Sunday of Ordinary Time (Mt 13:1-23)

REFLECTING

The Parable of the Sower in today's gospel is well known. It is a beautiful story which speaks of God's work in the world and the response of his people to that work.

Jesus likens the sower's seed scattered along the footpath, on rocky soil, among thorns and on good soil to four ways his message can be received: heard but not understood, joyfully welcomed but left to fade, heard but allowed to be overcome by distractions, heard and understood. We understand this parable, for do we not have each of these experiences at one or another time in our life? Do we not welcome the word of God in different ways at different times?

Yet what nobility is ours! Jesus calls our eyes and ears "blest" because they are capable of seeing and understanding the mystery of his kingdom. Indeed, the presence of God is a mystery that surrounds us, that penetrates our very being, that permeates all of creation. We must live with minds and hearts open to his beauty and truth around us. As his disciples, it is our *responsibility*, it is an obligation to welcome the word and in the word bear a fruitful harvest.

TALKING

1. Talk about ways in which God's word can yield a harvest.
2. Baptism plants the seed. Discuss how the other sacraments bring the seed to harvest.
3. Share your answers:
   I am like the seed on _____ because I _____.
   People do not accept Jesus because _____.
   To have an understanding heart, you must _____.

DOING

1. Picture Jesus leaving the house, walking to the lake, sitting down on the shore. See the people slowly gather. What kind of people come? What are they doing? Notice Jesus get up, walk to a boat, push out from shore. See the crowd stand along the shore. With them, hear Jesus tell the story of the sower. (One family member tells the story or the whole family pantomimes the story.)

2. Make your weekly scripture symbol—a bag of seeds. Place it in your home or on your SUNDAY THROUGHOUT THE YEAR banner.

PRAYING

"Blest are your eyes because they see and blest are your ears because they hear."

Lord,
Bless our eyes so that we can see your presence in others, in your creation, in your word.
(Make the sign of the cross on the eyes of each family member.)

Lord,
Bless our ears so that we can hear your word, your message, your Good News.
(Make the sign of the cross on the ears of each family member.)

Lord,
Bless our hearts so that we can understand your will in all that we do.
(Family members make the sign of the cross.)

16th Sunday of Ordinary Time (Mt 13:24-43)

REFLECTING

Jesus told many stories in the form of parables, a form which had been used for a long time in Israel and which was used during the time of Jesus by many Jewish rabbis. Jesus was a master of the parable and examples of his parables were preserved by oral tradition.

The parable is an indirect way of teaching a moral or religious lesson. Its purpose is to persuade us by having us reflect on our own daily experiences. So the parable begins with the things we know and touch in everday life.

In many of the parables we begin to understand the mystery of the kingdom of God. In the two parables of today's gospel we see the small beginning of the kingdom, the mustard seed and the yeast in the flour, and then the great growth, the big shrub where birds build their nests and the dough which rises in ferment.

The reign of God, the kingdom, can also be likened to a man who sows good seed in his field. In the same field, his enemy sows weeds. These are allowed to grow together till harvest for fear that in removing the weeds, the wheat may be pulled up with them. Like the seeds, we are to live side by side with unbelievers. But we must be cautious that we do not begin to accept the attitudes and lifestyle of the "weeds" as we live together till the harvest.

Besides telling us about his kingdom, these parables tell us about God. He is good, forgiving, patient, always ready to give us another chance. It is comforting to know that it is to this God we pray. And, as the second reading tells us, when we do not know what to pray for or what words to use, we simply let the Spirit of God within speak for us. How caring is our God!

TALKING

1. Talk about the kingdom of God parables. In round-robin fashion, name as many as you can.

2. What are some of the ways that we as a family can help the kingdom grow?

3. Share your answers:
   For me, a parable is _____.
   My favorite parable about God is _____.
   The reason Jesus used parables is _____.

DOING

1. Weed your garden. Experience the difficulty in pulling weeds around plants and leaving the plants intact. Make bread. Note what yeast does.

2. Make your weekly scripture symbol—a bird in a tree. Place it in your home or on your SUNDAY THROUGHOUT THE YEAR banner.

PRAYING

Lord,
With your Spirit, we can understand your word and we can speak our prayer. Thank you for telling us about your Father and his kingdom. Through your stories, we know we are invited to live this kingdom life. We accept your invitation. Together as a family, we will grow in the reign of God. Amen.

17th Sunday of Ordinary Time (Mt 13:44-52)

REFLECTING

The tin man in the Wizard of Oz tells us that life would be quite wonderful if he only had a heart. Without a heart, life has no meaning for him. His friends travel with him in search of the only person who can give him a heart, the Wizard.

The Lord offered Solomon anything he wanted (1 Kgs 3:5-12). Solomon did not ask for riches or a long life, but for an understanding heart. Like the tin man, Solomon knew that it is with the heart that one is able to judge right from wrong. It is the wise and understanding heart that brings peace and meaning into life.

An understanding heart welcomes the parables that Matthew tells of God's kingdom. In the parables of the buried treasure and the pearl of great price, we see two men rejoicing and willing to give up everything in order to make these finds their own. How impressed we are with their total commitment to possessing these objects. This is the way we too must live in the kingdom in order to possess the fullness of God's life.

Let us share our treasure, our pearls of great price, so that we can keep the faith alive and renew in one another the life of the kingdom.

TALKING

1. Discuss ways to know what is of worth. How do you make this judgment?
2. Talk about the Second Coming of Jesus in the fullness of time.
2. Share your answers:
   If I were Solomon, I would have asked for _____.
   With a buried treasure, I would _____.
   An object that means a great deal to me is _____ because _____.

DOING

1. Make up your own parable based on the importance of an object someone has found and the total commitment of the finder to keeping it.
2. Make your weekly scripture symbol—a buried treasure. Place it in your home or on your SUNDAY THROUGHOUT THE YEAR banner.

PRAYING

Lord,
Your kingdom is our treasure. We rejoice that we have found you. We place you first in our life.

Your kingdom is our pearl of great price. All that we are, all that we possess, we give to you. Give us a wise and understanding heart so that we will know what is right and choose your will in all that we do. Amen.

18th Sunday of Ordinary Time (Mt 14:13-21)

REFLECTING

Picnics remind us of summertime and of gathering together to celebrate. Can you imagine a picnic with 5,000 people present? One can almost see the variety of people and hear the sounds of happy interchange. One wonders what games the children played.

In today's gospel Jesus has withdrawn to a deserted place. After hearing of the death of John the Baptist, Jesus needed to be alone to pray. But the crowds followed him. Seeing their needs, he was moved with pity. Answering their needs, he cured the sick and healed the brokenhearted.

Night approached. Jesus assured the disciples that there was food enough to feed the 5,000. In the multiplication of the loaves and fishes we are reminded of the kindness, care and providence of God in giving manna to the people in the desert. We recall the gift of Jesus himself in the bread of the Eucharist, the gift which nourishes and strengthens us, the gift that will last forever, the only food gift that satisfies our spiritual hunger.

It is interesting to see how Jesus offered his disciples the opportunity of feeding, distributing, and then gathering the leftovers. They are involved in the process of life itself and in acting they began to understand the mission that was theirs.

As Jesus gave thanks to his father before he blessed the bread, so we give thanks to God for every meal we eat. God has formed us as a new people. This is what the kingdom is like, people living together in God's presence, receiving the abundance of his life.

TALKING

1. Talk about your favorite food, your favorite celebration. Reflect on the conversation at a meal with people who share what they have.

2. Talk about ordinary bread. Talk about the bread of the Eucharist which nourishes and strengthens us in our daily living.

3. Share your answers:
   I need you, God, I need you to _____.
   I am most thankful for _____.
   For me, a meal is _____; your meal of the Eucharist is
   _____.

DOING

1. Write a family meal blessing to be said every day this week.

2. Make your weekly scripture symbol—a picture of fish and bread. Place it in your home or on your SUNDAY THROUGHOUT THE YEAR banner.

PRAYING

Thank you, Lord.
Thank you for being in our life and answering all our needs.
Thank you for letting us know that the hungers of all your people are the same.
Lord, let us recognize your helping presence in our daily living.
"The hand of God feeds us; he answers all our needs" (Ps 145:15-16).

19th Sunday of Ordinary Time (Mt 14:22-33)

REFLECTING

In today's gospel we have one of the strongest confessions of faith by the disciples. Jesus showed mastery over the wind and the sea. Peter wanted this same mastery and in faith reached out to Jesus. He began to walk on the water. Suddenly he became crippled by doubt and fear and cried out to Jesus for help. Often we, too, are crippled by the storms in our lives. Like Peter, we have only to ask for help. And, in the quiet moments following the storms, we can exclaim with the disciples, "Truly, you are the Son of God!"

It is in the quiet and solitude of our own prayer moments that we express our faith in God. Both Elisha on the mountain praying and Jesus going up the mountain by himself to pray speak the need to balance active lives with quiet moments of prayer.

TALKING

1. Discuss ways to grow in faith.

2. Storms are a part of the inside life. How do you overcome them? Reflect on the meaning of fear in your life. How does it hamper you? Jesus said, "Do not be afraid." How does that make you feel?

3. Share your answers:
   If I had been Peter, I would have _____.
   The "mountain" where I go to pray is _____.

DOING

1. Act out this faith scene. Speak out your fears and proclaim your faith.

2. Make your weekly scripture symbol—a sign, "Be not afraid." Place it in your home or on your SUNDAY THROUGHOUT THE YEAR banner.

PRAYING

Lord,
Sometimes we are afraid, afraid of what others think and say, afraid of our limitations, afraid that we cannot be the person you call us to be.

Help us to be like Peter. Let us reach out to you in our fear, for we know you will heal us. Let us reach out to members of our family and with your help heal their fears.

In faith, let us meet you. Let us look at you and say, "I believe in you."

(Trace a cross of faith on the forehead of each family member and say: "Be not afraid. Jesus is with you.")

20th Sunday of Ordinary Time (Mt 15:21-28)

REFLECTING

In his inaugural address President Reagan told this story of Martin Treptow, a young man who was killed in World War I. On his body was found a diary with this pledge inside: "I will work, I will save, I will sacrifice, I will endure, I will do my utmost, as if the issue of the whole struggle depended on me alone."

We may not be called upon to make the ultimate sacrifice that this young man made, but like the woman of today's gospel we are asked to live with a pledge of faith, a consistent faith in making this old world into a new one.

This foreign woman was persistent in requesting that Jesus come and heal her daughter. Indeed, the apostles were embarrassed by her shouting. The woman accepted the fact that the Chosen People came before her, but she insisted on the blessing of Christ. For this blessing she was willing to endure, sacrifice and even accept the disciples' rebuffs.

Jesus' first response to the woman was silence, then conversation. Finally, in pity, he reached out to heal: "Woman, you have great faith. Let your wish be granted." The clear message of today's gospel is that God's love extends to all people.

Like Jesus, let us treat all people with charity and respect. Like Martin Treptow, let each of us in faith pledge to live our lives as if the whole struggle depended on us alone.

TALKING

1. Talk about belief. For what would you be willing to sacrifice your life?
2. Do determined people embarrass you? If so, in what way?
3. Share your answers:
   My response to this woman would have been _____.
   I am embarrassed when _____.

DOING

1. Practice saying, "Please, Lord," in your prayers this week. Like the Canaanite woman, speak with God from the depth of your needs.
2. Make your weekly scripture symbol—a sign of a woman with the word "Faith."

PRAYING

(Parents, extend your hands over the children. Children, bow your heads for God's blessing.)
Parents: May the Lord bless you.
Children: Amen.

Parents: May the Lord keep you.
Children: Amen.

Parents: May the Lord let his light shine on you and guide you and protect you.
Children: Amen.

Parents: May almighty God the Father, the Son and the Holy Spirit, bless you all forever.
Children: Amen.

(Trace the sign of the cross on the forehead of each child.)

21st Sunday of Ordinary Time (Mt 16:13-20)

REFLECTING

Balloting continued. Periodically, black smoke appeared from a chimney in the Vatican where the cardinals of the church had gathered. Suddenly, white smoke appeared and the cheers of the people in St. Peter's Square rang out, "We have a new pope. *Vive il papa!*"

From Peter, the rock of the church, the line of the papacy has continued down through the ages. There have been 262 popes in the Catholic church.

In today's gospel Jesus asked the disciples, "Who do people say the Son of Man is?" He received various answers: John the Baptizer, Elijah, Jeremiah, one of the prophets. Through these answers, Jesus discovered where the people were in their understanding of him. Then he asked Peter directly, "But you, who do you say that I am?" Peter answered, "You are the Christ, the Son of the living God." What a beautiful profession of faith by a man who would later deny that he even knew Jesus! We are all frail, yet Jesus chooses us as he chose Peter to continue his work in a particular way. To Peter he said, "You are Peter and on this rock I will build my church . . . I will give you the keys of the kingdom of heaven."

Let us recognize Jesus as Messiah, the Anointed One, and proclaim with Peter, "You are the Christ, the Son of the living God."

TALKING

1. Talk about the hierarchy in the church. Discuss the duties of the pope, cardinals, monsignors, bishops, priests, brothers, sisters and lay people.
    The bishop of my diocese is _____.
    My parish priest is _____.
2. Share your answers:
    Like Peter, I speak out and say _____.
    The title I use for the pope is _____.

DOING

1. Make a mobile of the different people who form the hierarchy of the church. Place their names on the figures and hang the mobile.

2. Make your weekly scripture symbol—a key. Place it in your home or on your SUNDAY THROUGHOUT THE YEAR banner.

PRAYING

(Concluding doxology of the Eucharistic Prayer)
Through him,
with him,
in him,
in the unity of the Holy Spirit,
all glory and honor is yours,
almighty Father,
for ever and ever.

(Respond to this prayer of unity as a family by singing the great Amen.)

22nd Sunday of Ordinary Time (Mt 16:21-27)

REFLECTING

Former hostage Kathryn Koop spoke of the daily routine she and Elizabeth Swift established for themselves while in Iran. "After breakfast in the morning, we spent the next few hours in prayer. We felt we needed to center our lives and to prepare ourselves to meet anything that could come our way during the day."

What is it that sustains us, that gives us the strength to get through difficult times? Jesus told Peter and the disciples that he was going to Jerusalem to suffer and to die. The values of life and love revealed and lived through his Father sustained Jesus through those difficult times.

If it was difficult for Peter to accept that Jesus was to suffer and die, how shocked he must have been when Jesus continued speaking: "If anyone wants to be a follower of mine, let him renounce himself and take up his cross and follow me." This is Jesus' challenge to each of us.

Jesus lived by God's standards. Sometimes we make life difficult for ourselves by conforming instead to the standards of the world. In the second reading, Paul tells us clearly not to conform to this age but to renew ourselves by seeking God's will, by doing what is good, pleasing and perfect for him.

TALKING

1. Consider what your children will say about what you have taught and lived. What will sustain them through the difficult times?

2. Talk about God's standards and the standards of this age. By which do you live? Are any of the standards the same?

3. Share your answers:
   I live through difficulties by _____.
   The family values that we live by are _____.
   Like Peter, I find it hard to accept _____.

DOING

1. As summer ends, take a family walk to praise and thank God for this season. Recall together your family moments of outdoor life.

2. Make your weekly scripture symbol—a sign of the cross. Place it in your home or on your SUNDAY THROUGHOUT THE YEAR banner.

PRAYING

Lord,
Place in our hearts a desire to please you in all that we do. Help us to grow in knowing you. Give us life and love to sustain us through the difficult times. Let us never work to gain the world—to be popular, intelligent, successful, secure—and ruin ourselves in the process. And Lord, please Lord, let us have no fear as we follow in your footsteps and take up our cross to come after you. Amen.

23rd Sunday of Ordinary Time (Mt 18:15-20)

REFLECTING

"I guess you can pray without comin' to church, Gran ... But I figure
that if you've got a whole churchful of people prayin' with you ...
you're gonna have a lot more clout."

—Comic strip *Quincy*,
Shearer

Our little friend Quincy has a good insight on the message of today's gospel: Join your
voices in praying and what you ask shall be granted to you. Jesus makes it clear that
whenever two or three are gathered in his name, he is there among them.

It is because of the presence of the risen Lord among us that we are not only able to
pray together but to live in community with one another. In community we work and
play, grow and share and recognize the presence of God in all that we do. Because of
his presence we have the power to settle our disagreements.

In the gospel Matthew offers a practical guide for handling disputes. When one person
offends or disagrees with another, they should sit down together and try to settle it.
If they are unable to agree, then they should invite a third party to sit and talk with
them. If an agreement still cannot be reached, then the matter should be brought to the
community.

Developing the art of resolving disputes will always be a challenge to each of us. We
should welcome the people that God has chosen to guide us. We should listen to their
voices without hardened hearts. Let us humbly learn the ways of community life, the
way of recognizing the presence of God among us. It is his presence that gives power
and life.

TALKING

1. What people serve as guides in your life? Share ways they have helped and continue
to help you.
2. Is the gospel's guide for settling disputes practical? How do you settle disagreements
in your family? Do you feel time will solve all problems and so remain silent? Or do you
feel it is better to clear the air by honest discussion, even if it is painful?

DOING

1. Develop a practical guide for handling and
resolving disagreements in the family. Post it where
everyone can see it.
2. Make your weekly scripture symbol—a series of
hearts. Place the symbol in your home or on your
SUNDAY THROUGHOUT THE YEAR banner.

PRAYING

Lord,
You offer us a challenge, a difficult challenge, in accepting correction from others, in
handling disagreements, in settling disputes. Sometimes the challenge is too difficult.
Sometimes pride and self-righteousness get in the way.

Help us to remember that it is your presence that gives us the ability to live in harmony with one another and to resolve difficulties. It is your presence that calls us to
pray together and to share your life.

Thank you for being with us. Amen.

(Turn to each family member and promise to begin to settle disagreements kindly
together.)

Sep 6, 1981 / Sep 9, 1984 / Sep 6, 1987

24th Sunday of Ordinary Time (Mt 18:21-35)

REFLECTING

"The quality of mercy is not strained,
It droppeth as the gentle rain from
      heaven . . .; we do pray for mercy
And that same prayer doth teach us
      all to render
The deeds of mercy."

—Portia in Shakespeare's *Merchant of Venice*

It is not easy to forgive. Our personal, family and business experiences have repeatedly shown us that forgiveness is not easy. We hesitate to live a life of mercy.

Peter asked a very human question: "How often must I forgive?" He probably felt generous when he suggested "As often as seven times?" Jesus' answer, "Not seven, I tell you, but seventy-seven times," meant an uncountable number. It conveyed clearly to his hearers that there must be *no* limit placed upon the number of times we are called to forgive.

The mercy of God does come as "gentle rain" upon all of us for all times. We are called to "render the deeds of mercy" to others. To make sure we understand this call for reconciliation, Jesus tells the story of the unforgiving servant. Our life in the kingdom of God consists in this: Because we are forgiven through the mercy of God, we must in mercy forgive others.

TALKING

1. Discuss ways we can overlook the faults of others.
2. Share your answers:
   For me, God's mercy is _____.
   As a sign of a healing church, I would _____.

DOING

1. Choose to forgive one person for whom you carry anger. Go to him or her personally and say you are sorry.
2. Make your weekly scripture symbol—a heart with "77" inside. Place it in your home or on your SUNDAY THROUGHOUT THE YEAR banner.

PRAYING

Leader: You were sent to heal the contrite:
      Lord, have mercy.
All: Lord, have mercy.

Leader: You came to call sinners:
      Christ have mercy.
All: Christ, have mercy.

Leader: You plead for us at the right hand of the Father:
      Lord, have mercy.
All: Lord, have mercy.

—from Penitential Rite C of the Mass

Sep 13, 1981 / Sep 16, 1984 / Sep 13, 1987

25th Sunday of Ordinary Time (Mt 20:1-16a)

REFLECTING

A gift that's freely given must freely be received. . . . All that we can offer you is thanks.

—the Dameans,
Beginning Today

The Parable of the Workers in the Vineyard tests our sense of fairness and challenges our understanding of justice. We may think of the work we do and the amount of money we are paid. It certainly strikes us as unjust that someone who has worked for only one hour be paid the same salary as another who has worked all day. We react against this unfairness.

If this parable is hard for us, how much more difficult it must have been for the Israelite people who had served Yahweh faithfully through the centuries. In their eyes, the Gentiles, all of us, had only begun to serve. Yet our reward will be the same.

When we listen to this parable through the person of the owner, we are able to understand it in a different way. The owner of the vineyard, like God, gives his gifts freely. There is nothing we do to merit the gift; we are called only to respond fully to the gift, to say yes or no. All that we can offer in return for the gift is thanks. The mercy of God to all his people, the outcasts, the rejected, the little ones, the late believers, is limitless. Because we are incapable of understanding the mercy of God, we should be careful not to impose limits on his relationship to his people.

We are not in competition with one another in our service to God. We should never be jealous over the gifts of others, but rather rejoice in the goodness that God has given them. We should live a life of thanksgiving daily.

TALKING

1. Talk about the way you feel when you are in an unfair situation. How do you handle these feelings?

2. Discuss jealousy. What do you do and how do you feel when you see the goodness in another in serving God?

3. Share your answers:
   I am most like the worker who was hired _____.
   God's generosity is _____.

DOING

1. Pantomime the gospel while someone narrates.

2. Make your weekly scripture symbol—a couple of coins. Place it in your home or on your SUNDAY THROUGHOUT THE YEAR banner.

PRAYING

Response: The Lord is good to all.
In our success and failure . . .
In our daily work at home, school, business . . .
In the gifts that make each of us special . . .
In our hopes and dreams . . .

Lord,
It is hard to find words of thanks for your goodness in our life, for the gift of yourself in our life. May we always experience and understand your limitless generosity toward all of your people. Amen.

CYCLE A

26th Sunday of Ordinary Time (Mt 21:28-32)

REFLECTING

> Shout for joy, you heavens . . .
> Shout aloud, you earth below!
> Shout for joy, you mountains,
> and you, forest and all your trees!
> For Yahweh . . . has displayed his glory.
>
> — *Isaiah 44:23*

How wonderful that we can shout "Jesus Christ is Lord!" We bow our heads; we bend our knees; we proclaim the name of Jesus. This is our faith, this is our belief, this is the glory of Jesus: He is Lord.

The irony is that in being Lord he became a servant. He became poor, humble, obedient to the will of his Father. He welcomed suffering and death. He became like us and calls us to become like him.

In the second reading we heard the words of St. Paul to the first church he established in Europe, "The attitude you should have is the one that Christ Jesus had . . ." (Phil 2:5). That is our call as well. In spite of our human failings, of our need to be recognized and honored, of our selfish interests and self-centeredness, we are asked to put on the mind of Christ, to accept his lifestyle, to welcome his values. To do all of this, we must become humble. We must look to the gifts of others and rejoice in these gifts. We must look to become servants of others and be joy-filled to serve.

TALKING

1. Talk about names. A name is powerful. What does your name mean?
2. List the different names for Jesus. Discuss the meaning of calling Jesus "Lord."
3. Share your answers:
   Like Jesus, I am obedient when I _____.
   I find it hard to serve when _____.

DOING

1. Write a letter of encouragement to a friend or relation as Paul did to his friends.
2. Make your weekly scripture symbol—a Chi-Rho. Place it in your home or on your SUNDAY THROUGHOUT THE YEAR banner.

PRAYING

(Whenever you hear or say the name of Jesus in this prayer, bow your head.)

Lord Jesus, (bow head)
you came to lead us to your Father, we praise you.

Lord Jesus (bow head)
you were obedient to the will of your Father, we bless you,

Lord Jesus, (bow head)
you became like us, and you call us to become like you, we thank you.

Come, Lord Jesus. Come in glory.

(Genuflect while making the sign of the cross.)

27th Sunday of Ordinary Time (Mt 21:33-43)

REFLECTING

My friend had a vineyard
on a fertile hillside.
He dug the soil, cleared it of stones,
and planted choice vines in it.
In the middle he built a tower,
he dug a press there too.
He expected it to yield grapes,
but sour grapes were all that it gave.

— Isaiah 5:1-3

The image of the vineyard has been used throughout the Old Testament. The vineyard is the people of Israel. God is the loving keeper of the vineyard. Jesus tells the parable of the tenants in allegorical form and invites the people to consider its meaning.

Just as the prophets were rejected by the people so, too, Jesus is "the stone the builder rejected." Two sets of servants (the major and minor prophets) are sent by the owner of the vineyard (God) to get the harvest. They are beaten, stoned and killed. Finally, the landowner sends his only son (Jesus). He, too, is taken outside the vineyard and killed.

In the loving care and protection of God, our landowner, we are asked to produce good fruit in our life by doing God's will in love and service to others. What kind of grapes have we produced? Are we *overripe*, still waiting to begin our work? Are we *sour*, afraid to show joy? Are we *colorless*, hesitant to use our talents and gifts? Are we like *wild* grapes, alone, separated from community, tasteless, preoccupied only with our own wants and needs?

TALKING

1. Talk about ways to be caretakers of the earth and her people.
2. Share your answers:
   I feel rejected when _____.
   As a "grape," I am _____.
   I produce good fruit by _____.

DOING

1. Place a bowl of grapes on the table. Make place cards for each family member. Draw a grape on each. Place them on the supper table.

2. Make your weekly scripture symbol—a bunch of grapes. Place it in your home or on your SUNDAY THROUGHOUT THE YEAR banner.

PRAYING

Lord,
May we never reject your presence in our life. Through our work and love, may we welcome all of your people into our life. Help us to be your vineyard and care for us always. Amen.

28th Sunday of Ordinary Time (Mt 22:1-14)

REFLECTING

WE REQUEST
THE HONOR OF YOUR PRESENCE
IN THE KINGDOM
OF GOD

God's invitation is generous. He invites all people, the good and the not so good, the loving and the not so loving. No one has earned a right to the invitation. It is simply given as a gift to everyone.

It seems unlikely that anyone would refuse this invitation. Yet, we do—at least some of the time. Someone needs to talk with us, but we are busy with our own work. Someone asks us to help, but we have another commitment. When we live a life that is self-centered, thinking only of what we need or of the things we have to accomplish, we fail to respond to the needs of God's people. We need all our time and energy for ourselves. "Sorry, I can't, I'm busy."

In today's gospel the invitation by a king to the wedding banquet of his son is dramatically refused and the people who bring the invitation (prophets and preachers) are rejected. Let us put on our wedding garment by living our baptism—putting on the mind of Christ, accepting his values and beginning to live his lifestyle. Only then can we live fully and joyfully with God forever in his kingdom.

TALKING

1. Talk about ways that make us unfit to come to a banquet.
2. Talk about the proper clothing to wear to the banquet.
3. Share your answers:
   When I spend too much time talking or thinking about myself, I feel
   _____.
   When someone asks me to help them, my immediate response is
   _____.
   When I am not invited to a party and my friends are, I _____.

DOING

1. Make a Chi-Rho for each family member. After the Chi-Rho's are used in Praying (see below), place them on bedroom doors.
2. Make your weekly scripture symbol—an invitation. Place it in your home or on your SUNDAY THROUGHOUT THE YEAR banner.

PRAYING

Lord,
Thank you for your invitation to live your life. We accept this invitation. We say yes. To show our acceptance, we receive and wear this sign of Christ.

(Call each person's name. Say, "You have been invited. Welcome Christ." Place a Chi-Rho on the person.)

May we offer one another some sign of congratulations for living the life of the kingdom.

(Give each other congratulatory signs: handshake, kiss, hug, etc.)

29th Sunday of Ordinary Time (Mt 22:15-21)

REFLECTING

In today's gospel Jesus tells us not to be distracted from the essentials of life. Though different groups desire to trick him, Jesus answers masterfully when questioned on whether or not one should pay tribute through taxes to the Roman ruler. He says that if you use Caesar's money, then you must expect to pay for it. It is interesting to note that Jesus did not even have a coin on him but had to ask that one be shown him.

We also must not be distracted from the essentials of life, from the heart of the matter. And the heart is this:

> Give back to God what belongs to him.
> Give him your mind
> your understanding
> your knowledge: All these belong to God.
> Give him the joy experienced in friends
> the peace experienced in friends
> the calm experienced in solitude: All these
> belong to God.
> Give him the work you have done
> the recognition you have achieved
> the honor you have received: All these belong
> to God.
> Give him the moments of family living
> the days of hoping and dreaming
> the years of faithfulness and promise: All
> these belong to God.

TALKING

1. Our basic need is to belong. Talk about the ways your family helps you to know you belong to them and they belong to you.

2. Reflect on your attitude toward your gifts.

3. Share your answers:
   I show I belong to God by _____.
   For me, the heart of the matter is _____.
   I am willing to give back to God _____.

DOING

1. As a family, list all the gifts that you have on a paper. Across the top of the paper write: "We give to God what belongs to him."

2. Make your weekly scripture symbol—a tax form. Place it in your home or on your SUNDAY THROUGHOUT THE YEAR banner.

PRAYING

(Pray today's Responsorial Psalm. Extend your hands forward, palms upward, for this prayer.)

"Give to the LORD, you families of nations,
   give to the LORD glory and praise;
   give to the LORD the glory due his name!" (Ps 96:7-8—NAB).

Thank you, God, for the ability to give. Thank you for letting us belong to you. We give you, God, all that is yours. We give you all of life. Amen.

Oct 18, 1981 / Oct 21, 1984 / Oct 18, 1987

30th Sunday of Ordinary Time (Mt 22:34-40)

REFLECTING

"I don't know. What should I choose? I can't make up my mind."

Decisions can be bothersome things. We make many decisions daily, ranging from the small and insignificant to those of ultimate concern. For many people, the making of a decision, the ordering of priorities, can be overwhelming.

The lawyer tried to trick Jesus with the question that people have long debated: Which commandment of the law is greatest? But Jesus refused to be placed in any specific school of thought that would answer *this* or *that* commandment. Instead, Jesus gave us the single commandment: Love God and love his people. He makes our decision-making process quite simple. Every decision that we make must be done in the light of whether it will help us to love God and his people more.

During this week we will celebrate All Saints' Day; we will honor all those men and women who faithfully loved God and his people throughout their lives. They are our models of behavior, people who made the decision to be directed toward God in all that they did and to be responsible for his people. May all our lives be based on love— a love of community and love of God in community.

TALKING

1. Talk about ways to put your love into action.
2. How do you make God the center of your life?
3. Talk about your name saint.
4. Share your answers:
   My most difficult decision was _____.
   My favorite saint is _____ because _____.
   As a reminder to turn to God, I would carry in my pocket
   _____.

DOING

1. Make hearts. Place them on all the mirrors in your home.
2. Make your weekly scripture symbol—a heart. Place it in your home or on your SUNDAY THROUGHOUT THE YEAR banner.

PRAYING

Lord,
Sometimes we fail to love,
we talk about our friends,
we turn away from those in need,
we become angry,
we act irresponsibly,
we forget to say, "I love you."

Help us to love you, Lord, with our whole heart, our whole mind, our whole soul, and to love our neighbor as ourself. Amen.

(Offer your family some sign of love.)

31st Sunday of Ordinary Time (Mt 23:1-12)

REFLECTING

> Live carefully. You may be the only gospel your neighbor ever reads.
> —author unknown

In today's gospel Jesus is clearly telling us to live carefully. What we preach we also must practice. It is in the way we live that the Good News is spoken.

We need never seek a name or title of honor or position of authority. We need not look holy and religious. We need only serve and carefully live a life of love for others.

The words of Jesus to those who do not practice what they preach are powerful and condemning. He says to listen to those who demand that others follow laws and teachings they pay no heed to themselves; but do not follow them. Listen to those who preach a life of caring for others, even though they never welcome the stranger, the homeless, the lonely into their own lives; but do not do as they do.

Hypocrisy is known to all of us: the mothers and fathers who ask of their children more than they themselves are willing to give, political and religious leaders who expound the principles of democracy or the teachings of the church but feel they are excused from practicing them themselves, all of us who know what is good and beautiful but decide not to live it.

There are many people in our lives whom we call holy. They live totally dependent upon God. God uses them to speak his word, to live his message. These men and women live carefully for they know God may intend that they be the only gospel their neighbor ever reads.

TALKING

1. Discuss ways to handle hypocrisy in your life.
2. Talk about the values of Christ you find most difficult to live.
3. Share your answers:
   To "live carefully," I _____.
   For me, hypocrisy is _____.

DOING

1. Make a tassel and hang it in your kitchen. Tassels were prescribed for the clothes of those who were pious. Jesus wore a tassel, but in a humble way.

2. Make your weekly scripture symbol—another tassel. Place it in your home or on your SUNDAY THROUGHOUT THE YEAR banner.

PRAYING

(Sit silently as a family. Think about the following line.) "Live carefully. You may be the only gospel your neighbor ever reads."

Pause. (Talk with God about how you feel about this. Listen. Thank God for his Good News and for calling you to live this news. Then hold hands and together say "Amen.")

32nd Sunday of Ordinary Time (Mt 25:1-13)

REFLECTING

There is great excitement in the planning of a wedding. So many things to do, food to order, clothes to be selected, guests to be invited. And what an honor to be a bridesmaid! Everyone together prepares for this celebration day.

Today we hear the story of the ten bridesmaids who were chosen for a place of honor at a wedding. According to a Palestinian marriage custom the bridesmaids stand with lighted lamps along the road. These lamps light the way for the arrival of the bridegroom.

In Matthew's gospel story there was a delay in the coming of the bridegroom (Christ). The bridesmaids (all of us) fell asleep. When the arrival of the bridegroom was finally announced, the bridesmaids who had brought enough oil for their lamps began their walk in a lighted procession. The foolish bridesmaids, perhaps forgetting why they had come, or taking too lightly the purpose of their coming, did not bring enough oil. The bridegroom welcomed the prepared, turned the foolish away.

Sometimes we are like the foolish bridesmaids. We have been given the invitation to come meet Jesus, and yet we do not prepare for this meeting. We forget that we will not even be able to recognize him in this meeting unless we have already met him in some way before—in our prayers, in the sacraments, in people, in the experiences we live.

TALKING

1. The motto of the Boy Scouts is "Be prepared." Talk about ways to live prepared lives.

2. In what signs do you recognize God in your life? Meeting Jesus daily helps one to be prepared to know him when he comes as bridegroom.

3. Share your answers:
   I am like the bridesmaid who _____.
   We welcome Jesus daily in our life by _____.
   In my life, I am most prepared for _____; least prepared for
   _____.

DOING

1. Place small "Get ready" signs on all the clocks in your home.

2. Make your weekly scripture symbol—an oil lamp. Place it in your home or on your SUNDAY THROUGHOUT THE YEAR banner.

PRAYING

(Become the bridesmaids by holding candles in a processional line.)

Response: Makes us ready for you, Lord.
We light our candles as a sign of our waiting in readiness for the coming of Jesus ...
Help us plan ahead and be organized in our daily work ...
Help us to be faithful in our words and to complete what we begin ...
Help us to live in welcome of your daily coming into our lives ...

33rd Sunday of Ordinary Time (Mt 25:14-30)

REFLECTING

All our gifts and talents belong to God. By using our gifts, we give praise and thanksgiving to God.

In today's gospel the attitude of the first two servants as well as the attitude of the wife in the first reading (Prv 31:10-13) is one of faithfulness. Here we see a fidelity in being who we are and in using responsibly the gifts that God has so generously shared with us.

How have we used the gifts God has given us?
IN OUR FAMILY—
Do we use our ability to listen?
Do we try to understand and answer the immediate needs of each family member?
IN OUR SCHOOLS OR BUSINESS—
Do we use our ability to act?
Do we try to do our best in all that we do?
IN OUR PARISH—
Do we use our ability to pray as a community?
Do we joyfully celebrate our Sunday Mass?
IN CREATION—
Do we use our ability to mend and fix things that are broken?
Do we respect and take care of all of nature?

We should consider always our state of preparedness for the Second Coming of Jesus by examining the way we are using our talents, his gifts to us.

TALKING

1. Talk about the different gifts you have as an individual and as a family. Be affirmative.
2. God shows his confidence and trust in us through his giving of gifts to each of us. Examine together the ways you have responded to this trust.
3. Share your answers:
   For me, fidelity to being who I am means _____.
   The gift I use most is _____.
   I give praise and thanksgiving to God by _____.

DOING

1. Make a family tree of gifts and talents. On the tree, have family members place their names and the names of the gifts they will try to use responsibly. Present this tree at your Thanksgiving meal as your thanksgiving prayer.

3. Make your weekly scripture symbol—a hand with the word "Gift" inside. Place it in your home or on your SUNDAY THROUGHOUT THE YEAR banner.

PRAYING

(Create an atmosphere of silence. Read the following words of scripture slowly.)

"You have shown you can be faithful in small things, I will trust you with greater; come and join in your master's happiness."

Talk with God about how you feel about these words (pause).
Listen (pause).
Resolve on the particular way you will be dependable this week (pause).
Thank and praise God for being present in your life.

Nov 15, 1981 / Nov 18, 1984 / Nov 15, 1987

Solemnity of Christ the King (Mt 25:31-46)

REFLECTING

To accept Jesus as our king, we must recognize ourselves as his subjects. To be a subject is to be docile, to follow the guidance of the king, to do his will. In this way we can begin to live in his kingdom forever.

As his people, the standard of entry into this kingdom is the mercy we show others. This kingdom is one of friendship and love where we celebrate Jesus in his people, his friends whom we serve. When we welcome the stranger, give drink to the thirsty, clothe the naked, comfort the sick or visit the imprisoned, we know Jesus. We recognize Jesus in his kingdom for we have known him already in his people.

Our liturgical year ends with this celebration of Christ as king. In this mystery, we his people proclaim his reign over all of creation. He is king of every heart and mind. He is king of all time and place. We help build his kingdom of truth and life, of holiness and grace, of justice, love and peace. One day we will be welcomed by Jesus, our friend and king, to live in this kingdom forever.

TALKING

1. How do you treat people who proclaim and live the gospel? With resentment? With jealousy? With rejection? What is your reaction when you see people helping others? Joy? Guilt? Do you think they are showing off? Do you belittle them to others?

2. Talk about ways to become a sheep, docile and humble to the will of the shepherd, Jesus.

3. Share your answers:
    I welcome the stranger by _____.
    I offer comfort by _____.
    I recognize Jesus as shepherd and king by _____.

DOING

1. Make a crown from a circle of paper. Place it in the center of the table. Choose one way you will try to help others this week. Write your intentions on a slip of paper and place it in the crown. Review it at the end of the week.

2. Make your weekly scripture symbol—a crown. Place it in your home or on your SUNDAY THROUGHOUT THE YEAR banner.

PRAYING

Leader: As king he claims dominion over all creation, that he may present to you, his almighty Father, an eternal and universal kingdom:
All: an eternal and universal kingdom:
Leader: a kingdom of truth and life,
All: a kingdom of truth and life,
Leader: a kingdom of holiness and grace,
All: a kingdom of holiness and grace,
Leader: a kingdom of justice, love and peace,
All: a kingdom of justice, love and peace.

Leader: And so with all the choirs of angels in heaven we proclaim your glory ...
All: Alleluia! Alleluia! Alleluia!
                    —adapted from the Preface for the Mass of Christ the King

Nov 22, 1981 / Nov 25, 1984 / Nov 22, 1987

CYCLE B

SUNDAY THROUGHOUT THE YEAR Banner—Cycle B

1st Sunday of Advent (Mk 13:33-37)

REFLECTING

Have you ever worked with clay? Can you recall the feel of the clay as you shaped and formed it? How did you, the potter, respond when you looked at your completed work, the work of your own hands?

As a people we are the clay constantly being shaped and formed into one people. Our potter is God. As clay welcomes the hand of the potter, so we offer ourselves to be molded by God. We stand with our heads high, confident, prayerful, persevering. As the work of God's hands, we try to live in hope and peace. We enjoy God's life in the present while we wait for the fullness of promise in the future, the fullness of what we are called to be as persons and as a people.

During Advent we celebrate comings, a long-ago coming of Jesus on Christmas day, a daily coming of Jesus into our hearts, and a future coming of Jesus at the end of time. For this coming, we know not the day or time. So together we must be on guard, constantly watching. We must stay awake so we are not taken by surprise.

If we, like clay, are allowing ourselves to be formed by the Potter, then we have already experienced God in our life. In that experience we have life. With his life we can await confidently and eagerly the Second Coming of his Son Jesus.

TALKING

1. Talk about the way Jesus comes daily into our hearts, our work, our neighbor.
2. Discuss: We are the clay; you are the Potter.
3. Share your answers:
   To prepare for Advent, our family will _____.
   To stay awake I will _____.
   As the work of God's hand, I feel _____ because _____.

DOING

1. During the next four weeks you will be praying the O Antiphons—names of praise for God traditionally prayed in the Advent season—during Praying (see below). Each week make and cut out a sign for the Antiphon to be prayed. Attach the sign to a stick (one about 8″ long works well). Decorate a flower pot, fill it with sand and place it in the center of the dinner table. You will place the sign in the flower pot during Praying.

This week you will be praising God under the name *Wisdom*. The sign for Wisdom is a bird or a God's-eye.

2. Make your weekly scripture symbol—a clay pot with the words, "Form us, O Lord." Place it in your home or on your SUNDAY THROUGHOUT THE YEAR banner.

PRAYING

Lord,
We praise you as *Wisdom*. You are forming us as your people. We are your clay. We await your coming in the fullness of time. Be our potter forever.
O Wisdom, who came from the mouth of the Most High, who reaches from end to end, who gives order to all things mightily and sweetly. Come and show us your wisdom.

(In a ceremony, place the sign you made in Doing #1 in your O Antiphon flower pot.)

Nov 29, 1981 / Dec 2, 1984 / Nov 29, 1987

CYCLE B

2nd Sunday of Advent (Mk 1:1-8)

REFLECTING

We are not alone in waiting and preparing for the coming of Jesus. People have walked this path before us. Isaiah is one of our faithful guides for this Advent season. Isaiah's songs and words offer hope and expectancy to us today just as they prepared the exiled people for their return home long ago.

The words of Isaiah in our first reading (Is 40:1-5, 9-11) are applied to John the Baptist in the desert. While wearing camel's hair clothing and eating grasshoppers and wild honey, John preached words of repentance. People flocked to listen to him, to confess their sins and to receive baptism in the Jordan River. John was relentless in preparing a way for the coming of Jesus; he was humble in recognizing that his cousin who was to come was far more powerful than he.

We are people called to hear the glad tidings that God is present in our life. In his presence we can live with an inner peace, joy and comfort. We can be at home wherever we are, for home means being with God.

TALKING

1. Talk about the people you know who have walked before you marked with the sign of faith. Plan to pray for them at Sunday Mass.
2. Discuss ways the family can prepare as Isaiah and John did for the coming of Jesus.
3. Share your answers:
   I know I am not alone when _____.
   For me, John is _____.
   I am at home with God when _____.

DOING

1. (If you have not read Doing #1 for the 1st Week of Advent, p. 71, do so now.) This week you will be praising God under the names *Lord and Ruler* and *Root of Jesse*. A burning bush or a tablet of law is a sign for Lord and Ruler; a flower is a sign for Root of Jesse.

2. Make your weekly scripture symbol—a road with the word "Prepare" on it. Place it in your home or on your SUNDAY THROUGHOUT THE YEAR banner.

PRAYING

Response: We will prepare your way.
I send my messenger before you . . .
A herald's voice in the desert crying . . .
Make ready the way of the Lord . . .
Clear him a straight path . . .

O Lord and Ruler of the House of Israel, who came to Moses in the burning bush, who gave Moses the Law on Mt. Sinai, come and redeem us.

(Place the sign you made in Doing #1 in the flower pot.)

O Root of Jesse, standing as a sign for all people, standing before the silence of kings, you to whom the Gentiles offer their prayers, come and deliver us. (Place the sign you made in Doing #1 in the flower pot.)

3rd Sunday of Advent (Jn 1:6-8, 19-28)

REFLECTING

> "Do you swear to tell the truth, the whole truth, so help you God?"
> "I do."
> The witness was questioned. His testimony before the court was
> recorded and heard by the jury.

Throughout the gospel of John, there are testimonies and witnesses. John the Baptist was questioned by the people: "Who are you?" Through his honest and humble response the people discovered that John was simply a herald, a proclaimer, a man called by God to alert the people to the presence of Jesus among them and to testify to that presence.

In his testimony, we see John's humility in recognizing and accepting his mission. John was called to be a witness to the light, but he was not the light. He announced the Messiah, but he was not the Messiah.

The people thought that perhaps John was Elijah, the prophet, who was expected to return before the day of the Lord. They were wrong. John was not Elijah. The people had been told to anticipate a prophet like Moses whom they were to obey. John was not this prophet either.

John reveals himself as "a voice": "a voice that cries in the wilderness: Make a straight way for the Lord."

Like the people, we too wait for the one who is to come on Christmas day.

TALKING

1. How do you give testimony to the presence of Jesus in your life?
2. Consider the questions you would have asked John. Give a profile of John.
3. Share your answers:
   To make straight the way of the Lord, I would _____.
   I am sent by God to _____.

DOING

1. (If you have not read Doing #1 for the 1st Week of Advent, p. 71, do so now.) This week you will be praising God under the names *Key of David* and *Dawn of the East*. A key is the sign for Key of David; a rising sun is the sign for Dawn of the East.

2. Make your weekly scripture symbol—a lamb carrying a banner. This is the traditional sign for John the Baptist. Place it in your home or on your SUNDAY THROUGHOUT THE YEAR banner.

PRAYING

O Key of David and Scepter of the House of Israel, who opens and no one closes, who closes and no one opens, come and free us.

(Place the sign you made in Doing #1 in the flower pot.)

O Dawn of the East, brightness of light eternal, sun of justice, come and bring us your light.

(Place the sign you made in Doing #1 in the flower pot.)

Dec 13, 1981 / Dec 16, 1984 / Dec 13, 1987

CYCLE B

4th Sunday of Advent (Lk 1:26-38)

REFLECTING

>Welcome, God. Be with me as I study and work. Let me always be
>surprised by your presence.

A young girl wrote the above words in her prayer journal. One can only wonder about the situation which prompted the expression of these sentiments to God.

We need not wonder, however, about Mary's words in response to the announcement of the angel Gabriel. Her simple "Yes" changed the world. With that response Mary welcomed God in a special way into her life. Her yes is the yes we can say daily as we welcome Jesus into our lives.

Mary was a woman of faith. She believed in God and in the wonderful things he had done for his people. She remembered Abraham, Moses, Deborah, David and all the men and women throughout history that God had chosen to help the people keep their faith in him.

In joy, Mary rejoiced in the goodness of God in sharing his life with us. Loved by God, we, too, rejoice in his coming and in gladness welcome him into our lives.

TALKING

1. Talk about past and present events in your life that bring you joy.
2. Discuss ways you can live the "Yes" of Mary in your own life.
3. Share your answers:
   I welcome God into my life by _____.
   As a person of faith, I remember these people who prepared for Jesus' coming:
   _____.

DOING

1. (If you have not read Doing #1 for the 1st Week of Advent, p. 71, do so now.) This week you will be praising God under the names *King of Nations* and *Emmanuel*. A crown is the sign for King of Nations; a crib is the sign for Emmanuel.

2. Make your weekly scripture symbol—the word "Yes." Place it in your home or on your SUNDAY THROUGHOUT THE YEAR banner.

PRAYING

Response: Pray for us.
Holy mother of God . . .
Mother of Christ . . .
Cause of our joy . . .
Morning star . . .
Mother of peace . . .
Mother of light . . .
And Mary, thank you for saying "Yes."

O King of Nations, the desired one, our cornerstone, you who will bring all people together, come and make us one.

(Place the sign you made in Doing #1 in the flower pot.)

O Emmanuel, our king and ruler, you are the expected one of all people, the savior for all nations.

(Place the sign you made in Doing #1 in the flower pot.)

Feast of the Holy Family (Lk 2:22-40)

REFLECTING

In order to fulfil the requirements of the Jewish Law, Mary and Joseph took Jesus to Jerusalem to present him to the Lord and also to offer sacrifice. What must Mary and Joseph have thought when Simeon took the child Jesus in his arms and said:

> "Now, Master, you can let your servant go in peace,
> just as you promised;
> because my eyes have seen the salvation
> which you have prepared for all the nations to see..."

Then he blessed them and said,

> "You see this child: he is destined for the fall and for the rising of
> many in Israel, destined to be a sign that is rejected—and a sword will
> pierce your own soul too—so that the secret thoughts of many will
> be laid bare."

Jesus is indeed our salvation. Through him we are to reach the glory of eternal life. But we are also asked to follow him, and his path leads to the cross before it reaches resurrection.

The holy family returned to Nazareth after this experience in the Temple. There "the child grew to maturity, and he was filled with wisdom; and God's favor was with him." May our families provide us with opportunities for growth in spiritual maturity and wisdom and give us the affirmation and support we need to follow Jesus through the cross to glory.

TALKING

1. How do you feel when someone in your family is praised by others? How do you feel when a member of the family is rejected?

2. Is your family a place where each member can grow to maturity and be "filled with wisdom"? Why or why not?

3. Share your answers:
   I accept Jesus when I _____.
   I reject Jesus when I _____.

DOING

1. As a family, plan a visit to church. Present yourselves to the Lord and offer a sacrifice—perhaps money you have saved by giving up a treat—by leaving an offering for the poor.

2. Make your weekly scripture symbol—a pair of doves in a cage. Place it in your home or on your SUNDAY THROUGHOUT THE YEAR banner.

PRAYING

Father in heaven ...
In history's moment when all was ready,
you sent your Son to dwell in time,
obedient to the laws of life in our world.

Teach us the sanctity of human love,
show us the value of family life,
and help us to live in peace with all men
that we may share in your life for ever. Amen.

—from the alternative Opening Prayer for the
Mass of the Holy Family

Dec 27, 1981 / Dec 27, 1987

Feast of the Baptism of the Lord (Mk 1:6b-11)

REFLECTING

> I don't know who—or what—put the question. I don't know when it
> was put. I don't even remember answering. But at some moment I did
> answer Yes to Someone—or Something—and from that hour I was
> certain that existence is meaningful, and that therefore, my life had a
> goal.
>
> —Dag Hammarskjold

Baptism offers us a meaningful existence. Through baptism we too say "Yes to
Someone." We say yes to welcoming God into our lives; we say yes to being formed as
the people of God, brothers and sisters calling God our Father.

Jesus came to the Jordan to be baptized by John. Today's first reading (Is 42:1-4, 6-7)
speaks of the servant whom God has chosen and loves. At his baptism Jesus is marked
as this servant, the servant who will proclaim and suffer. The dove—the Spirit—
descends as a sign of God's love.

The dove also represents the new people of Israel. The final age has begun. A new community is beginning with the Spirit to give it life. This promise will be fulfilled at
Pentecost when again the heavens will be opened and the Spirit will come to all those
present.

Through our baptism we become part of this Spirit-filled community. Through this life-
giving power, we continue to unfold as God's people.

TALKING

1. Talk about the need for the Spirit in your life.
2. To what do you say yes? How does that yes give meaning to your life?
3. Share your answers:
   I offer my family this sign of love: _____.
   For me, baptism is _____.

DOING

1. Write the date of each family member's baptism
and the name of his or her godparent on your
calendar. Plan to celebrate each anniversary. Invite
the godparents to the celebrations or send a thank-
you notes and offer special prayers for them.

2. Make your weekly scripture symbol—a dove
under water. Place it in your home or on your
SUNDAY THROUGHOUT THE YEAR banner.

PRAYING

(Renew your baptismal mission as you listen prayerfully to the words of the signing of
the senses.)

Receive the sign of the cross on your ears:
may you hear the voice of the Lord.
Receive the sign of the cross on your eyes:
may you see with the light of God.
Receive the sign of the cross on your lips:
may you respond to the word of God.
Receive the sign of the cross on your breast:
may Christ dwell in your hearts by faith.
Receive the sign of the cross on your shoulders:
may you accept the sweet yoke of Christ.
> —from the Rite of Christian Initiation of Adults

Jan 10, 1982 / Jan 13, 1985 / Jan 10, 1988

2nd Sunday of Ordinary Time (Jn 1:35-42)

REFLECTING

"Any telephone messages?" you ask as you walk into your home.

There is one illegible scribbled message. You call the doubtful number.

"Did you call me?" you ask.

A voice replies, "No, sorry, it must have been someone else."

It is frustrating not to know who has called you.

Young Samuel must have felt this same frustration. He heard his name called many times and each time he was curious to know who had spoken his name. His friend, Eli, helped him discover the identity of the caller. The caller was God.

In our first reading (1 Sm 3:3-10, 19), we hear that Samuel was not familiar with the Lord and so did not recognize his call. John the Baptist, however, recognized Jesus as the Lamb of God and Andrew proclaimed to his brother Peter that in Jesus he had found the Messiah. Will we recognize Jesus? How long will it take for us to become familiar with the Lord?

God knows each of us by our name. As we slowly grow to know him, our reply to his call in our life may echo the reply of the young boy, Samuel: "Speak, Yahweh, your servant is listening." And in listening we will see Jesus as the Lamb of God and recognize him as the Messiah.

TALKING

1. Talk about ways to know the Lord, to become more familiar with him.

2. Share a time when a friend, like Eli, helped you by telling you what to say or do in a difficult situation.

3. Share your answers:
   When someone calls me by my name, I feel _____.
   I listen to God when I _____.
   I am most like Samuel when I _____.

DOING

1. Have family members place their names on their bedroom doors as a sign that they are called by God.

2. Make your weekly scripture symbol—a conversation balloon with the words "God calls." Place it in your home or on your SUNDAY THROUGHOUT THE YEAR banner.

PRAYING

(Family members genuflect on this response:)

Response: Here I am, Lord, I come to do your will.

Lord,
I want to get to know you better, and I say . . .
I want to learn to listen carefully to your call, and I say . . .
I want to help my friends, and I say . . .

Thank you, God, for coming into my life as you came into young Samuel's life. Be with me in all that I do. Help me and give me the strength to be able to always say . . .

Jan 17, 1982 / Jan 20, 1985 / Jan 17, 1988

CYCLE B

3rd Sunday of Ordinary Time (Mk 1:14-20)

REFLECTING

"We have lived here for many years. Perhaps we should move to a new location and find new jobs and a new lifestyle. We need a family vote. How many are willing to move?" This is not an easy decision to make. Hesitantly, some hands may be raised. Most of us are reluctant to change our way of living.

Yet this is what Jesus asked of the brothers Simon and Andrew and the brothers James and John in today's gospel. Fishing was their life. When Jesus asked them to follow him, they immediately put aside all that was comfortable to them, all that they loved. They must have been afraid to begin a new occupation. But how quickly they responded to the words of Jesus!

In today's first reading (Jon 3:1-5, 10), the prophet Jonah was sent by God to the wealthy city of Nineveh to ask the people to change their way of living. Jonah walked through Nineveh proclaiming his message of repentance. The people listened. They were sorry for their sins and began to fast. To show their sorrow and to do penance, they took off their rich clothes and put on sackcloth. They changed their lives.

Like the people of Nineveh, like the fishermen, we are called to change, to repent and to welcome the message of the Good News. We must give our immediate response. Jesus does not always ask us to change our occupation, but he does ask that we change our way of living into his way of living. With God's mercy, we know this is possible.

TALKING

1. Talk about the feelings of the fishermen as they left their fishing nets. Share your feelings on beginning a new occupation or lifestyle.

2. Share a time you listened to someone, as the people of Nineveh did, and changed your ways. How did you show this change?

3. Share your answers:
   To have a change of heart, to repent, I would _____.
   I am most like Jonah when _____.

DOING

1. Write "Hear ye, hear ye," on a heavy piece of paper. Have each family member write one way he or she will try to change during the week. Post the intentions and proclaim them each night at dinner.

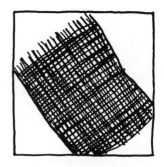

2. Make your weekly scripture symbol—sackcloth. Place it in your home or on your SUNDAY THROUGHOUT THE YEAR banner.

PRAYING

Lord,
It isn't easy to change. To begin a new way of living takes courage. To wear sackcloth and ashes is to show a change of heart, to show that we have listened to the Good News and are willing to turn away from our selfish way of living. It is your love and mercy that helps us to change. Help us, Lord, to reflect your love and light, your mercy and goodness to others. Amen.

Jan 24, 1982 / Jan 27, 1985 / Jan 24, 1988

4th Sunday of Ordinary Time (Mk 1:21-28)

REFLECTING

"If no one knows, no one gets hurt. Besides, I only needed that one answer."

"Everyone else is doing it. Anyway, I didn't have the money for the record and I wanted it."

Sometimes we hurt others and we hurt ourselves by lying, cheating and stealing. Through these actions, we do not allow ourselves to be the persons God calls us to be. If Jesus were walking our street or visiting our school, home or place of business, how would we explain these actions to him? Would we be like the man with the unclean spirit in today's gospel who shouted: "What do you want with us, Jesus of Nazareth? Have you come to destroy us?"

We live in an instant culture. What we want, we want immediately. We confuse needs and wants. We think people are not hurt by our actions because we cannot directly see that hurt. Have we lost our sense of justice, of respect for what belongs to others or is due others? Have we lost the ability to work for the things we want?

Jesus spoke sharply to the unclean spirit within the man: "Be quiet! Come out of him." We must respond to this order also by giving up the work of the unclean spirit—lying, cheating, stealing. Heed the sharp words of Jesus and follow his authority and not your own or the world's.

TALKING

1. Discuss the occasions of lying, cheating and stealing in your community. Role play these situations. Give reasons for your actions. How do you think these actions hurt others as well as yourself?

2. Offer solutions to the following dilemmas:

You and your friend are in a store. Your friend steals something. What do you do?

You need another can of paint for your kitchen. The store owner is out and a young assistant is unsure of the price. He says he thinks it might be $5. You know the price is $9. What do you do?

3. Share your answer:
For me, stealing is _____.
I want _____; I need _____.

DOING

1. During night prayers, think of the ways in which your actions during the day could have hurt others directly or indirectly. Privately make and post a list of no mores (for example, lying, cheating, stealing).

2. Make your weekly scripture symbol—a picket sign with the slogan "No more." Place it in your home or on your SUNDAY THROUGHOUT THE YEAR banner.

PRAYING

Lord,
We need your help. Help us to have courage to turn back to you when we have done wrong. Help us to seek friends who strengthen us as persons and who avoid hurting others. Help us to choose Christian values and to live those values. Help us to see you in others so that we never hurt them by lying, cheating or stealing.

We know what you want of us, Jesus of Nazareth. With one another, we will continue your work and live your life. Amen.

Jan 31, 1982 / Feb 3, 1985 / Jan 31, 1988

CYCLE B

5th Sunday of Ordinary Time (Mk 1:29-39)

REFLECTING

"I wish I had time to pray."

How often have we heard or said words like these? In today's gospel we see a typical day in the life of Jesus: hard work and prayer. In his work he healed Peter's mother-in-law and the many ill people who were brought to him. He preached the Good News. He went off to a lonely place to pray and, through prayer, to renew himself. The apostles sought him out and asked him to return quickly to the village where the people needed him. Like Jesus, we fill our lives with doing and praying. Like Jesus, we will be asked to respond to the needs of others.

Jesus felt the need for prayer in his life. We too need quiet moments to remember who we are, why we are. We need to set aside time—time to turn to God and to seek his presence, time to renew and grow in our friendship with him.

Prayer is talking with God, listening to God. Prayer can be formal, like saying the Our Father or the Apostles' Creed; it can be informal, speaking with God in our own words. Prayer can take the form of asking, thanking, praising, saying we are sorry. We can pray together or we can pray alone. Even our works can be a form of prayer.

TALKING

1. Discuss: "Prayer does not change God, but it changes the one who offers it" (Kierkegaard).
2. When is the best time for you to pray? Best place?
3. Share your answers:
    In my work, I pray _____.
    Alone, I pray _____.
    My favorite prayer is _____.

DOING

1. Make a prayer card. On top of the card, place the words "We pray for:" Fold the card and place it on the table as a centerpiece. Add the names of people in need to the card during the week.

2. Make your weekly scripture symbol—a hand with the words "We pray." Place it in your home or on your SUNDAY THROUGHOUT THE YEAR banner.

PRAYING

(As a family, pray this vocation prayer of John Henry Newman.)

God has created me to do him some definite service;
He has committed some work to me which he has not committed to another.
I have my mission ...
I am a link in a chain,
a band of connection between persons.
He has not created me for nought.
I shall do good. I shall do his work.
If I am in sickness, my sickness may serve him;
in perplexity, my perplexity may serve him;
if I am in sorrow, my sorrow may serve him.
He does nothing in vain,
He knows what he is about. Amen.

Feb 7, 1982 / Feb 10, 1985 / Feb 7, 1988

6th Sunday of Ordinary Time (Mk 1:40-45)

REFLECTING

I have all the moments of my life to give to you. Whatever I am thinking, whatever I am doing, however small, however insignificant, I do for you. Every moment comes to me, passes from me and goes into eternity, there to remain what I have made it. There is only one business that I have. I must hold myself to the present moment and let God act. In every moment that I live, God speaks.
—*Present Moment*, a reflection film, Ikonographics

Our lives are filled with things to do. Whether young or old, rich or poor, today's second reading (1 Cor 10:31-11:1) tells us how we are called to live: "Whatever you eat, whatever you drink, whatever you do at all, do it for the glory of God." Paul spoke these words to the people who lived in the busy, affluent, crowded town of Corinth. How appropriate they still are for us today!

The opening reflection echoes the sentiments of St. Francis de Sales. Through his writings he conveys that whatever we are doing, whatever we are thinking, however small and insignificant, must be for God. Through us his glory will be reflected around the world.

TALKING

1. Name 10 things you do in one day. How often do you remember to do those things for God? What helps you to remember?

2. Jesus reflected God's glory by what he did and said, by the way he lived. Talk about ways he remembered his Father in all that he did.

3. Share your answers:
   For me, the present moment is _____.
   My response to the words of Paul is _____.
   To help me remember to do all for God, I will _____.

DOING

1. Make a magazine collage of people doing things. Print across the top of your collage: "All we do we do for you, God."

2. Make your weekly scripture symbol—an hour glass with the Chi Rho on it. Place it in your home or on your SUNDAY THROUGHOUT THE YEAR banner.

PRAYING

Response: All we do, we do for you.
Whenever we are working at home, at school, at our job . . .
Whenever we are playing football, basketball, tennis, soccer . . .
Whenever we are laughing, crying, talking, listening . . .
Whenever we are eating breakfast, lunch, supper, a snack . . .
Whenever we are forgiving ourselves, people who have hurt us, those whom
    we have hurt . . .
Whenever we are loving to our mothers, our fathers, our sisters, our brothers, our
    friends, ourselves . . .

Thank you, God, for all the moments of our lives, moments in which to do your will, to show your glory. Help us to know your presence in all the present moments that we live. Whatever we do, we do for you. Amen.

Feb 14, 1982 / Feb 17, 1985 / Feb 14, 1988

7th Sunday of Ordinary Time (Mk 2:1-12)

REFLECTING

Friends are important people. They are with us in good times and times that are not so good. Friends are the caring, helping people in our lives.

In today's gospel four friends showed their loyalty by carrying their paralyzed friend to see Jesus. Not only did they carry the stretcher through the crowded streets, but, unable to reach Jesus, they climbed the roof of the house where Jesus was staying. On the roof, they removed a section of the straw covering and gently lowered their friend inside.

How happy Jesus must have been in seeing the faith of these friends! It is faith that gives us the courage to stand before God, to meet him as a friend, to ask and receive forgiveness and healing. To the paralytic Jesus said, "My child, your sins are forgiven." Sin and sickness are linked together not because one is a consequence of the other, but because both are signs of death. Sin cripples us.

Then, to show his authority to forgive sins, Jesus also cured the man physically: "I order you: get up, pick up your stretcher, and go off home." How happy his friends must have felt as they watched the man begin his walk home carrying his stretcher!

TALKING

1. Discuss ways friends are important in your life. Have family members share one way in which a friend has helped them during the past week.

2. Talk about the healing that comes from the sacrament of reconciliation. How is faith related to forgiveness?

3. Share your answers:
   Like the paralyzed man, I would _____.
   Jesus astounds me when he _____.
   As a scribe, I would have thought _____.

DOING

1. Give each family member a small piece of paper and a pencil. Have each person complete the following sentence: A friend is ... Place the papers in a container. Have each person draw one slip, read it aloud, and have the family try to guess the author.

2. Make your weekly scripture symbol—a mat or stretcher with the words, "Go home." Place it in your home or on your SUNDAY THROUGHOUT THE YEAR banner.

PRAYING

(As a sign of faith, stand for the following prayer.)

Response: We stand; we pick up our mat; we go home to live your life.

Give us faith, Lord, in your healing power ...
Make us joyful in the celebration of your forgiveness of our sins ...
Give us friends who turn us to you when we are in need ...
Make us bold, Lord, so that we have the courage to ask for your mercy ...

(To proclaim your faith and show your need for forgiveness, pray an Act of Contrition together.)

Feb 21, 1982

1st Sunday of Lent (Mk 1:12-15)

REFLECTING

The little boy tugged at his father's coat and pleaded, "But you promised, you have to, you just have to."

How many times have we heard these words or said them ourselves? Promises are sometimes hard to keep. There are circumstances that can force us to postpone or change the promises we have made to our children, our spouse or our friends.

In today's first reading (Gn 9:8-15), we hear of a promise God has made to us. "There shall be no flood to destroy the earth again." The rainbow is the sign that reminds us of that promise.

Jesus, too, made a promise. He promised to send the Spirit. The promise and the Spirit are one.

How wonderful to know that God always keeps his promises!

During this Lent, let us travel together on our faith journey and have renewed hope in the promised life.

TALKING

1. Talk about your promises you have made and kept and promises that have been made to you and kept. How do you heal broken promises?
2. Why do you think God chose a rainbow as a sign of his promise?
3. Share your answers:
   As a promise maker, I will _____.
   When a promise is broken I feel _____.
   At my baptism I promised _____; at confirmation, I promised
   (will promise) _____.

DOING

1. As a family, write your Lenten resolutions as promises. Renew these promises throughout Lent.
2. Make your weekly scripture symbol—a rainbow. Place it in your home or on your SUNDAY THROUGHOUT THE YEAR banner.

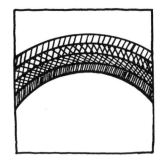

PRAYING

Lord,
You call each of us to become a promise-maker. May we keep your word in all that we do. We become like you when we make and keep a promise.

As our parents and godparents signed us with the cross on our forehead during our baptism, so we trace this cross on the forehead of one another and say: (*Name*), live the life of promise this Lent.

Help each of us to live your promise in our own unique way and together to have renewed hope in the promised life. Amen.

Feb 28, 1982 / Feb 24, 1985 / Feb 21, 1988

CYCLE B

2nd Sunday of Lent (Mk 9:2-9)

REFLECTING

The mountain has often been the meeting place between God and his people. Moses received the Ten Commandments on the mountain; on the mountain Elijah found God in the gentle breeze. Now Jesus brings Peter, James and John to the mountain. There he is transformed; his clothes become a brilliant white. There he speaks with Moses and Elijah. From an overshadowing cloud God's voice speaks: "This is my Son, the Beloved. Listen to him."

The awe and wonder of the three apostles soon changed to confusion as Jesus asked them not to speak of the experience until the Son of Man was raised from the dead. How can a Messiah suffer? Why would he freely choose to suffer? Like the apostles, we do not understand. But we too try to hold and remember this glimpse of the fullness of God's life in Jesus as we travel together the road from slavery to freedom, from death to new life.

TALKING

1. Talk about ways of seeing that are beyond just looking. What do we "see" in the Transfiguration?
2. Share the ways you listen to God in your life. Talk about prayer as listening.
3. Share your answers:
   I find it hard to listen to God when _____.
   The "mountain" where I pray the best is _____.
   The thing I find most difficult to understand is _____.

DOING

1. Set aside a few minutes each day for quiet meditation on scripture—a peaceful time to listen to what God is saying to you.

2. Make your weekly scripture symbol—a mountain with a cloud. Place it in your home or on your SUNDAY THROUGHOUT THE YEAR banner.

PRAYING

Response: We will listen and hear your voice.
In our frustrations and disappointments ...
In our happiness and joy ...
In our play and work ...
In our quiet and noisy moments ...

God,
In all that we do, let us seek your presence. Help us to grow in faith, to be filled with wonder and awe in the life of your Son.

In all that we do, we will listen. We will hear your voice. Amen.

(Sign the ears of each person and say:)

Receive the sign of the cross on your ears: may you hear the voice of the Lord.
—from the Rite of Becoming Catechumens in the
Rite of Christian Initiation of Adults

3rd Sunday of Lent (Jn 2:13-25)

REFLECTING

"I will do this for you, and you must do this for me." History has seen many of these political compromises. Some of them are remembered; some are not.

But there is one agreement—an agreement of friendship made long ago—that is still important for us. In the first reading (Ex 20:1-17), we hear God tell the people who he is and what he has done in delivering them from their Egyptian slavery. In this friendship treaty he asks for loyalty; he asks that the people remain faithful to him by living the gift of the Ten Commandments.

Through Moses, the people accepted the Ten Commandments. The first three commandments told them how to show their love for God; the remaining seven spoke of the way to act with one another. The commandments are our gifts, too. All of them are rooted in the singular command of God's covenant, the command to love.

During Lent we celebrate our entry into a new time, a new age. We are asked to have an unusual view of the world, an inner view which sees that following the law on the *outside* is not enough. To keep our part of the agreement with God we must be changed *inside*. We must be converted. We must decide to accept the message of Jesus and to accept the community which belongs to him.

It is during Lent that we ask ourselves if we are living the gift of the Ten Commandments. Are we showing our love for God and for his people? If we are not, then Lent becomes our time to change.

TALKING

1. As a family, talk about a positive action you can do in response to each commandment.
2. Discuss a friendship treaty. How is this type of treaty different from political treaties?
3. Share your answers:
   I will make this friendship agreement with God: _____.
   The easiest commandment for me to follow right now is _____.
   The commandment I find most difficult is _____.

DOING

1. As a family, write and display a friendship letter to God. Thank him for what he has done for you. Write what you will do for him. Have all the family members sign their names. Seal this treaty by eating together (a ritual practiced following the signing of treaties in ancient times).
2. Make your weekly scripture symbol—a tablet of stone for the Ten Commandments. Place it in your home or on your SUNDAY THROUGHOUT THE YEAR banner.

PRAYING

You are the Lord, our God. You have always been faithful to your people. We want to be faithful to you. You have asked that we follow you, that we follow the message of your Son. Help us to turn to you in all that we do. Help us to turn to your people and help them. Help us to turn inside so that we may change.

May we remember that you have promised that you shall be our God and that we shall be your people.

Mar 14, 1982 / Mar 10, 1985 / Mar 6, 1988

CYCLE B

4th Sunday of Lent (Jn 3:14-21)

REFLECTING

"Would you please turn on the light. It's dark in here."

"Yeah, we can't see a thing."

Sometimes our world is dark. We need someone to give us light, so we can see the goodness and beauty of all that God has made.

Jesus is the *light*. God so loved the world that he gave his only Son to us that we might see and believe. Just as Moses *lifted up* the serpent of bronze so that all who had been bitten by the serpents could look and live, so we too look at Jesus who has been *lifted up*, and we believe. Through faith we live in the light and we avoid darkness.

God's love for those who believe in his Son is boundless. Through faith we have a new birth in water and the Holy Spirit. In today's gospel Jesus tells Nicodemus about this new life.

Let us renew our faith and proclaim our belief in Jesus. Let us prepare now to renew wholeheartedly our baptismal promises during the Easter Vigil.

TALKING

1. As a family, talk about your beliefs. Discuss ways to grow in these beliefs.
2. Share your answers:
   I show I live in the light by _____.
   As Nicodemus, my response to the words of Jesus is _____.
   As the Light of the World, Jesus _____.

DOING

1. Smile and say hello to everyone on the way to and from work or school. Be reminded of God's love for all people.
2. Make your weekly scripture symbol—a candle with a heart on it. Place it in your home or on your SUNDAY THROUGHOUT THE YEAR banner.

PRAYING

(Place a lighted candle in the center of the table.)

Jesus,
You are the Light of the World. You came as a gift from your Father to help us see and believe. Help us to receive your light and to become a light to others. Amen.

5th Sunday of Lent (Jn 12:20-33)

REFLECTING

In today's gospel Jesus tells the apostles that his time has come:

> "Now the hour has come
> for the Son of Man to be glorified.
> I tell you, most solemnly,
> unless a wheat grain falls on the ground and dies,
> it remains only a single grain;
> but if it dies,
> it yields a rich harvest."

The seed must be put into the ground and covered with earth before it can grow and produce. As the seed, Jesus must first die in order to have new life and give new life to others: ". . . it was for this very reason that I have come to this hour."

When we die to selfishness, when we put away our old selves, we too become like the grain of wheat—we grow into new life.

TALKING

1. Talk about the process of seeding, growing and harvesting. Why do you think Jesus chose the grain of wheat as a sign?

2. Relate the story of the caterpillar, a creature that has to die in order to be reborn as a beautiful butterfly. Talk about the change from selfishness that each of us must make to be reborn as butterflies, free and beautiful.

3. Share your answers:
   To glorify God's name I will _____.
   To die to selfishness, I will _____.

DOING

1. Grow some wheat. (Pet stores sell wheat growing kits for about a dollar. The kit produces a crop of wheat in only a few days.)

2. Make your weekly scripture symbol—grain of wheat. Place it in your home or on your SUNDAY THROUGHOUT THE YEAR banner.

CYCLE B

PRAYING

Dear Jesus,

You have asked each of us to become like a grain of wheat, to die to selfishness in order to have new life. How hard this is! It is so easy to be concerned simply about our own needs and forget to serve others through their needs.

Lord, you have asked us to serve as you served. Like you, we are troubled. It is not easy for us to die to self. But our hour has come to change, just as your home came to die. With your help, may we put away our old life and begin to live a new life with you.

Your friends,
(Each family member says his or her name.)

Passion Sunday (Mk 14:1-15:47)

REFLECTING

> We adore you, O Christ, and we bless you,
> Because by your holy cross you have redeemed the world.

The apostles refused to see or understand Jesus' hints that he was to be a suffering Messiah. We can imagine the grief and confusion in the apostles' hearts as Jesus walked the road to Calvary. They were asked to walk that road too—and so are we.

Today we remember and celebrate what Jesus has done for us. He gave his life so that we could be free—free to love ourselves, free to love God and his people. The sorrowful mysteries of the Rosary commemorate five events in the passion of Jesus: Jesus prays in the Garden of Gethsemane; Jesus is whipped and beaten; Jesus is crowned with thorns; Jesus carries his cross; and Jesus dies. In each of these events, Jesus asks us to be with him.

We can see our own response to Jesus in the passion story, and we can find our own stories told in the individuals whose lives touched his. Through the kindness of the anointing woman, in the greedy Judas, in the denying Peter, in those people who accept or reject Jesus, in the obedient or abandoning disciples, in the helping Simon of Cyrene, in the cruelty of some of the soldiers, in the condemning crowd, in the women who stood by the cross, in the bold Joseph of Arimathea, we discover ourselves.

Forgive us for our failures, Lord, and grant us the strength to always follow you.

TALKING

1. Recall a past event in your life which filled you with sadness or confusion. Try to recall the cause of your feeling, the people present, what was said or done. How does your experience compare with those of other family members?

2. Talk about the different people present in this passion narrative. Who are you most like? least like? Why?

3. Share your answer:
   For me, the cross is _____.
   The one event in the passion that parallels my life today is

   _____.

DOING

1. Cover all the crosses in your home with purple cloth.

2. Make your weekly scripture symbol—a cross with the *INRI* (the Latin initials which stand for *Jesus of Nazareth, King of the Jews*). Place it in your home or on your SUNDAY THROUGHOUT THE YEAR banner.

PRAYING

(Say the following prayer together.)
We adore you, O Christ, and we bless you,
Because by your holy cross you have redeemed the world.

(Meditate in silence for a few moments. Then genuflect and make the sign of the cross.)

2nd Sunday of Easter (Jn 20:19-31)

REFLECTING

> Be patient toward all that is unsolved within your heart, and try to
> love the questions themselves.
> Do not seek the answers which cannot now be given you because you
> would not be able to live them, and the point is—to live everything.
> So, live the questions now. And perhaps you will gradually, without
> noticing it, live along some distant day, into the answer.
> —Rainer Maria Rilke

In today's gospel we see a man who was not at all "patient toward all that is unsolved." Thomas not only wanted answers, he wanted proof. When the apostles told him, "We have seen the Lord," Thomas responded, "Unless I see . . . I refuse to believe."

How like Thomas we are! We insist on proof. We refuse to cast our doubts aside and believe. Like Thomas we ask for signs and wonders; we close our ears to the testimony handed down to us.

And yet Thomas, the man of doubts, became Thomas, the man of faith. Once convinced, he expressed the most complete faith of anyone in the entire gospel, "My Lord and my God!"

Faith is a gift of God. By this gift we are already living the only beatitude that John mentions in his gospel: "Happy are those who have not seen and yet believe." Let us profess our faith in Jesus, the risen Lord. Let us say with Thomas, "My Lord and my God!"

TALKING

1. Do you think it is easier to believe today or during the days of the apostles? Why?

2. Talk about your doubts. What questions remain unanswered for you? How are you able to love the questions and profess your faith through them?

3. Share your answers:

I am most like doubting Thomas when I _____.

I am most like faith-filled Thomas when I _____.

I profess my belief in Jesus by saying _____.

DOING

1. Make a scroll. Across the top write "We believe." Have each family member design, color and post his or her name on the scroll. Display the completed scroll in your home.

2. Make your weekly scripture symbol—a question mark. Place it in your home or on your SUNDAY THROUGHOUT THE YEAR banner.

PRAYING

Lord,
Sometimes it is hard to believe. I lose faith in myself, in others, and even in you. I want proof, proof that you are with me, proof that you love and care for me. How foolish I am. Let me know your peace and joy so I can stand in faith and proclaim your goodness to the world. Help me believe in you and in all the people you have made.

(Turn to each family member and say: "I believe in you.")

Apr 18, 1982 / Apr 14, 1985 / Apr 10, 1988

3rd Sunday of Easter (Lk 24:35-48)

REFLECTING

"But I told you I would be home before dinner time."

The worried mother breathes a sigh of relief on hearing her child's voice.

How often we worry and doubt the words of another! Our doubts increase when the person is no longer with us, no longer able to reassure us.

We should easily understand the fears and doubts of the disciples of Jesus. Not only were they afraid that they too might be put to death, but they were also disturbed by the stories they had heard of the appearances of the risen Lord. Were the stories true? Was it possible that he was alive? What had happened on the road to Emmaus? How had the two disciples recognized Jesus in the breaking of the bread?

In today's gospel Jesus makes his final post-resurrection appearance. To convince the disciples he is not a ghost, he eats a meal of grilled fish with them. How much we are able to learn of another during our own meals! How much we learn of Jesus in the meal of the Eucharist!

Jesus showed himself to his friends not only to prove his resurrection but also to convince them to go out and preach his message. To be a witness to the resurrection event, we must not only believe but spread that belief. With the disciples, let us recall the words he spoke and pray that our minds will always be open to understand his word.

TALKING

1. What do you do when you are in a worrisome situation? Do you talk about your doubts? How do you handle them?

2. How do you show others that you believe in Jesus? How are you a witness to the Resurrection?

3. Share your answers:
   I am like the worried disciples when I _____.
   A meal convinces me that _____.
   The doubts in my heart are _____.

DOING

1. Make a magazine-picture collage of people in the world who live as witnesses to the Resurrection.

2. Make your weekly scripture symbol—a grill with a fish. Place it in your home or on your SUNDAY THROUGHOUT THE YEAR banner.

PRAYING

Response: We will not be afraid.
For the times it is difficult to tell the truth ...
For the times we have to meet new people and new situations ...
For the times we have to show who we are and what we believe ...
For the times we have to help those in need ...

Lord,
We are sometimes afraid as your friends were. Help us to overcome our fear and to remember that you are with us in all that we do. Let us experience your peace through doubting and frightening situations. As you offered peace to your friends, so we offer a sign of your peace to one another.

(Share a sign of peace with one another.)

4th Sunday of Easter (Jn 10:11-18)

REFLECTING

HELP WANTED

One shepherd—dangerous occupation, no personal gain, concern only
for others, no wages, willing to sacrifice for others, willing to risk life.

We can be sure there would be few applicants for this job! How many people are uninterested in personal gain? How many are willing to sacrifice their own interests for the welfare of others? Where are people eager to work for no wages?

In today's gospel Jesus is presented as the model shepherd. The way he lived his life totally for others offers the ideal for us. He was even willing to lay down his life for the sheep in his charge.

The good shepherd not only risks his life to protect his sheep, but he comes to know his sheep; he spends time with them, guides them, answers their needs. Not only does he know each of them by name, but they know him.

We are the sheep of a good shepherd. With Jesus as our guide, we are asked by God to help all people return home to the one fold.

TALKING

1. Talk about your work. In what ways are you able to show concern and care for others? Discuss your work ethic.

2. Recognizing the voice of God in our culture is difficult. Discuss the voices that call you away from God. What voices offer guidance and good direction?

3. Share your answers:
   As a sheep, I follow Jesus by _____.
   The model, the good and ideal shepherd, offers _____.

DOING

1. Outline a sheep on cardboard. Fill in the outline with cotton balls. Across the top of the cardboard write, "Jesus knows me." Hang it in your home.

2. Make your weekly scripture symbol—a shepherd's crook. Place it in your home or on your SUNDAY THROUGHOUT THE YEAR banner.

PRAYING

(As a family pray and reflect on Psalm 23:1-4.)

Yahweh is my shepherd,
  I lack nothing. (Pause)
    Lord, you are my shepherd and my friend. Give direction to my life.
In meadows of green grass he lets me lie.
To the waters of repose he leads me;
  there he revives my soul. (Pause)
    Lord, you nourish and re-create me. You bring comfort to my troubled heart.
He guides me by paths of virtue
  for the sake of his name. (Pause)
    Lord, I am lost sometimes. Help me to know your will.
Though I pass through a gloomy valley,
  I fear no harm;
beside me your rod and your staff
  are there, to hearten me. (Pause)
    Lord, you are always with me. Without you I could do nothing. Thank you for being the good shepherd in my life. I will be one of your sheep forever. Amen.

May 2, 1982 / Apr 28, 1985 / Apr 24, 1988

5th Sunday of Easter (Jn 15:1-8)

REFLECTING

Can you name one person who offers hope to you? Do you have a friend who makes you feel good about being you? Do you work more diligently and play more joyfully when you are with certain people?

Everyone needs the proper environment in which to grow and to live the fullness of life. To create this, we are asked not only to live for others but to *free* others to live.

Jesus has formed his people with his own life:
> "I am the true vine."

As his people, we live in him:
> "Whoever remains in me, with me in him,
> bears fruit in plenty."

A branch cannot produce fruit alone. As Christians we work with others in Christ to bear fruit. If we do not produce fruit together, we will be pruned from the vine. Without the vine, there is no life.

Through Christ's own glorified life, we produce joy, confidence, hope, love, trust. In this atmosphere, others are freed to live and to "bear fruit in plenty."

Jesus told his disciples to bring his message to others. This is the work of all who received life through the Resurrection. It is through our fruitbearing work that the Father is glorified.

TALKING

1. Talk about the ways in which your presence could help another work more diligently or play more joyfully.

2. Jesus has said, "I am the Resurrection and the Life," "I am the true Vine," "I am the Bread of Life." How do we partake in his life in each of these?

3. Share your answers:
   As the vine, Jesus _____.
   As the branch, I _____.
   To bear fruit in plenty, we _____.

DOING

1. Draw a vine on a piece of cardboard. Cut our leaves from construction paper. Have each family member write his or her name on one side of the leaf. On the other side write ones specific activity that he or she will carry out this week in order to "bear fruit in plenty." Paste the leaves, intention side down, on the vine. Hang in the kitchen.

2. Make your weekly scripture symbol—a vine with fruit. Place it in your home or on your SUNDAY THROUGHOUT THE YEAR banner.

PRAYING

Response: We are the branches of the vine.
May we give comfort to the lonely and the fear-filled ...
May we offer hope to the disappointed and rejected ...
May we build self worth in the doubtful and despairing ...
May we bring joy to the sad and depressed ...

Lord,
You are the vine in whom we have our life. Help us not only to bring your message of life to others, but to free others in choosing to live your life. And, Lord, let us work together as your branches in bearing fruit in plenty. Amen.

May 9, 1982 / May 5, 1985 / May 1, 1988

6th Sunday of Easter (Jn 15:9-17)

REFLECTING

"Mom, look, I am drawing a picture of God."

"But no one knows what God looks like," responded the mother.

The child handed her the drawing of a heart.

In today's second reading (1 Jn 4:7-10), we are presented with the deepest mystery of our faith: God is love. We learn of this love through the Son. We come to know God when we love.

In today's gospel Jesus speaks of the deep love he has for his disciples:
"As the Father has loved me,
so I have loved you."

So deep is his love for us that he calls us friends and offers us a dignity beyond our expectations:
"This is my commandment:
love one another,
as I have loved you."

To even consider that we have the power and the capacity to love in this way is staggering.

We are called to become lovers. Love is willing the best for another person. Love is communicating with another. Love is a commitment to be with and for other people. Love is a sharing of joy, interest and understanding. Love is union.

But can we really define the love of which John speaks? This love (agape) has its beginning in God. Love, then, consists in this: not that *we* have loved God but that *he* has loved us. How astonishing and overwhelming to be loved by him and to be called to love as Jesus loves!

TALKING

1. As a family, list the words that come to mind as you hear the word "Love."

2. Do you think it is important to love yourself? (Does the overwhelming fact that God loves you help you to answer this question?)

3. Share your answers:
God's gift to us is his son; my gift to God is _____.
I show my love for my friends by _____.

DOING

1. Give a surprise gift to someone you love; for example, cook a special meal for the family, babysit free, send notes to all your relatives.

2. Make your weekly scripture symbol—a heart. Place it in your home or on your SUNDAY THROUGHOUT THE YEAR banner.

PRAYING

Dear God,
Thank you for loving us. Thank you for giving us the ability to love you, others and ourselves. When we love, we come to know you better.

Sometimes it is hard to love. Sometimes people do not love us as much as we love them. Help us to remember your love for us. Help us to love all the people you have made and to show that love to them.

(To each family member say: (*Name*), I love you. Thank you for loving me.)

May 16, 1982 / May 12, 1985 / May 8, 1988

CYCLE B

7th Sunday of Easter (Jn 17:11b-19)

REFLECTING

One hundred and twenty disciples had gathered to await the coming of the Holy Spirit so they could begin their work in the world. One of the things they wanted to do was to choose a new apostle to replace Judas and restore the number of apostles to 12.

Today's first reading (Acts 1:15-17, 20a, 20c-26) describes the selection of the new apostle. Two qualifications were necessary: first, he had to have been with Jesus from the beginning of his public life; second, he had to have experienced the risen Lord, that is, he had to be a witness of Jesus' resurrection. Two men were nominated: Matthias and Barsabbas. Lots were drawn and Matthias was chosen.

In today's gospel Jesus prays to his Father for his disciples. This beautiful prayer is for us as well. He concludes with these words:

> "As you sent me into the world,
> I have sent them into the world,
> and for their sake I consecrate myself
> so that they too may be consecrated in truth."

Although we can not be one of the 12 apostles, we too have been chosen to go into the world and proclaim the truth, the Good News of Jesus. Let us go together!

TALKING

1. Pretend your family is a club. What qualifications are important for membership in this "club"?

2. Share your answers:
   In my life, the coming of the Spirit means _____.
   With the Spirit I will go into the world and _____.

DOING

1. The original novena is based on the nine days from Ascension Thursday to Pentecost. This was traditionally a time of prayer and expectations. Write a short family prayer and say it together daily as you await the coming of the Spirit.

2. Make your weekly scripture symbol—straws for drawing lots. Place it in your home or on your SUNDAY THROUGHOUT THE YEAR banner.

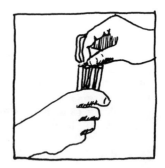

PRAYING

(Sit silently for a few moments as one family member reads today's Gospel Acclamation.)

Alleluia. The Lord said: I will not leave you orphans.
I will come back to you, and your hearts will rejoice (Jn 14:18). Alleluia.

(Say the prayer you wrote for Doing #1.)

May 23, 1982 / May 19, 1985 / May 15, 1988

Trinity Sunday (Mt 28:16-20)

REFLECTING

"I am going to give joy to all the people," said one child.
"I am going to bring love," said a mother.
"I am going to spread peace," said a father.
All the children and mothers and fathers went into the world to tell
the people about the Father and the Son, and the gift of the Spirit was
with them in all that they did.
The *Father* had told the secret:
   You must first love the king
   and then love the people as much as you love yourself,
   and the kingdom shall be yours forever.
The *Son* had lived the secret.
The *Spirit* helped the people remember and live the secret.
—from the Kingdom Series,
Ikonographics

In full authority, Jesus summoned the apostles to the mountain, the traditional place of revelation. In reverence they bowed down before him as they received his command to go into the world to preach and baptize all people in the name of the Trinity. His promise to be with them is still realized today in our own lives as we go forth in his name.

TALKING

1. Discuss ways to give joy, bring love, spread peace, and become a gift to one another. How do you live the secret of the kingdom?

2. Talk about Jesus' relationship to the Father and the Holy Spirit. In what prayers and in what gestures do you show reverence and acceptance of the Trinity in your life?

3. Share your answers:
   With the Spirit, I will go into the world to _____.
   One sign of unity in our family is _____.

DOING

1. Draw a picture of a town with people. Across the top of picture, print "I am going to bring:" In a balloon above each person's head, write what that person will do. Include family members in the town.

2. Make your weekly scripture symbol—a triangle (traditional symbol for the Trinity). Place it in your home or on your SUNDAY THROUGHOUT THE YEAR banner.

PRAYING

Father,
You sent your Son and, together in mutual love, the Holy Spirit. May we show reverence to you by genuflecting and making the sign of the cross:
   In the name of the Father
   and of the Son
   and of the Holy Spirit ...

(Bless each family member with water and the sign of the cross on the forehead.)

CYCLE B

Jun 6, 1982 / Jun 2, 1985 / May 29, 1988

Solemnity of Corpus Christ (Mk 14:12-16, 22-26)

REFLECTING

On the night before he suffered,
Seated with his chosen band,
Jesus, when they all had feasted,
Faithful to the law's command,
Far more precious food provided:
Gave himself with his own hand.

—Pange Lingua,
St. Thomas Aquinas

In celebration of the feast of Corpus Christi, Thomas Aquinas wrote these lyrics for plain song (chant). He also wrote the office prayers for this feast; they are considered by many to be the most beautiful in the breviary. We remember St. Thomas for his theological works, and now we have a glimpse into his poetic and prayer life.

Corpus Christi means "Body of Christ." In today's gospel we are told of the arrangements that were made for Jesus to celebrate Passover with his "chosen band." Following his instructions, two disciples found a room, spacious and furnished. In this room they prepared the Passover supper. During this meal Jesus gave us the gift of himself in the Eucharist.

Like the apostles, let us celebrate and receive the gift of Christ himself in the meal of the Eucharist. Let us sing songs of praise and thanksgiving.

TALKING

1. With family members reflect on your participation, celebration and reception of the Eucharist.

2. Recall different songs written in honor of the Eucharist. What is your favorite? Why? Choose one song and talk about its words.

3. Share your answers:
   For me, the feast of Corpus Christi is _____.
   My prayer of thanksgiving is _____.
   If I had been at the Passover meal, I _____.

DOING

1. Bake bread. Share your loaf with one another.

2. Make your weekly scripture symbol—a loaf of bread. Place it in your home or on your SUNDAY THROUGHOUT THE YEAR banner.

PRAYING

Lord Jesus,
We are one. We are your people.
Bless our homes with your presence.
Bless our hearts with your love.
Bless our hopes and dreams and joys.
Bless our family with good health.
Bless each room of our home.
Bless all places where we live.

(Bless your home. Sprinkle each room with blessed water.)

11th Sunday of Ordinary Time (Mk 4:26-34)

REFLECTING

"Be patient. God hasn't finished with me yet." So reads the caption on a popular poster. One can almost hear the pleading words of the young girl pictured on the poster.

These words capture the heart of one of the kingdom parables from today's gospel. A seed is planted in the ground. It grows slowly until time for harvesting.

God's kingdom is also unfolding slowly. We are asked to be trusting and patient. In due time the work of the kingdom will be completed.

Sometimes it is hard for us to remember that it is God's work we do and not our own. We do not control the growth of the kingdom; God does. We do not bring about the kingdom; God does. But we are asked to be active, not passive, in doing God's work.

As God's kingdom slowly unfolds, so does each person in the kingdom. Each of us slowly becomes the person God calls us to be. It takes a lifetime to become a person. Not only must we be patient with others, but patient with our own slow unfolding.

Let us continue to do God's work in building his kingdom. Let us be patient and trusting. God hasn't finished with us yet.

TALKING

1. Talk about the people in your life who call forth your best. Share ways you can offer patience and trust in helping others to slowly become the person God calls them to be.

2. Discuss with the members of your family the work you think God wants you to do in building his kingdom.

3. Share your answers:
   For me, the kingdom of God is like _____.
   I am not patient when _____.
   As a seed, my growth is _____.

DOING

1. Make a poster that reflects the themes of patience and trust in the slow unfolding of God's kingdom.

2. Make your weekly scripture symbol—a bag of seeds. Place it in your home or on your SUNDAY THROUGHOUT THE YEAR banner.

CYCLE B

PRAYING

Lord,
We are small. Sometimes we think we are insignificant. But then we remember the tiny mustard seed and its growth. We remember also that it is your power within us that calls us forth; it is your inner power in the world that calls the kingdom forth.

Time passes so slowly sometimes. We don't seem to be growing. Our lives do not reflect your presence. Forgive us for our lack of patience and trust in ourselves, in others and in you. Give us the strength to do your work in making this old world into a new one. Thank you for calling us to life in your kingdom. Amen.

12th Sunday of Ordinary Time (Mk 4:35-40)

REFLECTING

Sudden winds can come up on the calmest of lakes. A squall can develop within minutes. The force of the wind and waves can frighten even the best sailors.

In today's gospel story we see seasoned fishermen terrified by the waves and the winds. They rushed to the stern where Jesus was sleeping, awakened him and pleaded with him to save them. To the wind Jesus said, "Quiet now"; to the waves, "Be still." Turning to his friends he asked: "Why are you so frightened? How is it that you have no faith?"

Though the apostles were afraid, we must applaud their dependence upon Jesus, their immediate turning to him when they were in need. In our need, to whom do we turn? In our fears, upon whom do we depend? When we are under stress, how long does our faith last?

From this miracle we learn to trust in God's protection. As Jesus safeguarded the boat from harm, so also will he watch over and preserve his church, all of his people.

Filled with wonder and awe, the apostles asked one another, "Who can this be?" Through faith, we know the answer. He is our Lord, our lifesaver. With the wind and the sea, with all people of all time, we obey him.

TALKING

1. Share with family members an event or situation in which you experienced fear. How did you handle this fear? To whom did you turn for help?

2. Talk about miracles. In what way do they help you to believe?

3. Share your answers:
   For me, God's power is shown through ⸺⸺⸺⸺⸺.
   I am filled with wonder and awe when ⸺⸺⸺⸺⸺.
   A miracle is ⸺⸺⸺⸺⸺.

DOING

1. Pantomime this gospel story. Use a tambourine for the wind and wave sounds. Have family members share their feelings before, during and after the storm.

2. Make your weekly scripture symbol—a boat. Place it in your home or on your SUNDAY THROUGHOUT THE YEAR banner.

PRAYING

(Ask one family member to read slowly the following, pausing frequently:)
Close your eyes. Become quiet.
Picture a lake scene. There are a few boats on the lake.
See Jesus and his friends get into one of the boats and leave the shore.
Smell the calm lake water.
Feel the pleasant breeze.
Experience the comfort of the boat ride.
See Jesus asleep with his head on a cushion.
Place yourself in the boat. Are you standing? Sitting? Alone? With someone? Talking? Listening?
Suddenly the sky darkens and the winds rage.
Feel the wetness of the waves.
In fear, experience the rocking of the boat.
Ask Jesus for help.
Listen to his reply.
Thank God for his presence in your life.

Jun 20, 1982 / Jun 23, 1985 / Jun 19, 1988

13th Sunday of Ordinary Time (Mk 5:21-43)

REFLECTING

All of us have found ourselves in impossible situations. What should we do? To whom should we turn? Jesus gives us the answer. We can trust in him. When our world seems upside down, when we seem unable to do anything right, when we are afraid of what tomorrow may bring, we can trust in him.

Faith in Jesus brings healing and life. The worried father, Jairus, bowed before Jesus and asked him to heal his 12-year-old child. "Do come and lay your hands on her to make her better and save her life." Kneeling on the dusty ground before Jesus, Jairus spoke a beautiful prayer for help. And Jesus answered his plea.

May we too reach out in trust to Jesus and welcome his healing presence into our lives.

TALKING

1. In what ways have you been healed? What part did your faith have in this healing?
2. Talk about death as a part of life, as a step to the fullness of life.
3. Share your answers:
   I find it hard to trust when _____.
   In the sacrament of anointing of the sick, we _____.

DOING

1. Have family members write a prayer for help. List your worries and concerns. Print **HELP** in bold letters at the end.

2. Make your weekly scripture symbol—a hand with the words "Trust me." Place it in your home or on your SUNDAY THROUGHOUT THE YEAR banner.

PRAYING

Lord,
The people at Jairus' house did not have his faith. They laughed at you. I might have laughed, too. Like them I sometimes forget that you have the power to heal, that you have the gift of life, the life that goes on forever.

Give me trust, Lord. Give me faith in you. Make me sensitive to the needs and hurts of others. Use me to bring comfort, understanding and healing to a troubled world.

(Anoint the hands of each family member with oil, saying, " (Name) , be healed and go forth to heal others.")

CYCLE B

14th Sunday of Ordinary Time (Mk 6:1-7)

REFLECTING

A large, colorful "Welcome home" sign stretched across the street. People held pennants expressing welcome. The high school band played. Suddenly the streets were filled with confetti as the lead car drove by with the hometown celebrity. All the people of the town had gathered for this homecoming celebration.

Not everyone who returns to his or her hometown receives such a welcome, however. When Jesus returned to his hometown of Nazareth, the people were amazed at his wisdom and by the stories of the miraculous deeds he had performed. But this amazement soon turned to scepticism; their admiration soon changed to resentment. They could not understand how the simple son of a carpenter, one of their own townspeople, could possibly be so remarkable.

How disappointing! Are these not the very people—neighbors, friends, relatives—who should be eager to affirm and support the prophet?

Are we like the townspeople? Do we refuse to applaud the gifts of others? Do we emphasize the weaknesses of others with unkind words while we discount their strengths? Do we give someone a hero's welcome and then dismiss the person for failing to live up to our expectations?

The local people's lack of faith distressed Jesus. What about our lack of belief in others? Our jealousy of their gifts? Our lack of appreciation for the work they do?

TALKING

1. How do you show welcome and support to leaders and prophets in your own community?

2. Share ways to affirm the gifts of others, to build up the spirit within them. Begin with your own family members.

3. Share your answers:
    Like the townspeople, I am amazed at the way Jesus _____.
    I promise to support the prophet in my life by _____.
    I applaud the gift of _____ in _____.

DOING

1. Make and display a "Welcome home" sign in your kitchen. Place the names of your family members and members of your community on the sign to show your willingness to recognize and affirm their gifts.

2. Make your weekly scripture symbol—a pennant with the word "Welcome" on it. Place it in your home or on your SUNDAY THROUGHOUT THE YEAR banner.

PRAYING

Lord,
Send more prophets into our life. We will not despise them. We will welcome them as your people and rejoice in them as your gift to us.

Let the prophets among us never know rejection or ridicule, but only our support and love. Let us rejoice in their gifts and publicly proclaim and celebrate those gifts.

We welcome you, Jesus. We are your townspeople now. May we always show and live our faith in you and in one another. Amen.

15th Sunday of Ordinary Time (Mk 6:7-13)

REFLECTING

All the guests had arrived; the party was in full swing. There was good food and lively conversation. One young woman had a knapsack on her back. When someone asked why she wore it and what she had in it, she replied: "I want to be ready to go at a moment's notice—any place at any time. Inside are the things I would need for the journey."

This situation actually happened. Although somewhat eccentric for our world today, the young woman's readiness and her knapsack recall for us the expectancy and simplicity in which we are called to live. In our first reading (Am 7:12-15), Amos is called by God to leave his sheep and sycamore trees and go preach to the northern kingdom. Amos goes willingly and eagerly.

In our gospel reading, the apostles are called by Jesus to leave their nets and go forth to heal the people. Their immediate and eager response: Yes. How quickly the apostles responded! Their actions reveal a total dependence on God as they began their training program for ministry.

Amos and the apostles had no background experience for their work. Amos was not welcomed by the prophets of his day; the apostles knew only the sea and fishing. Yet even when Jesus intimated that they would be rejected in some places, they still went forth eagerly, totally depending upon God.

We, too, are called by God. How eager are we in our response? How trusting are we?

TALKING

1. Pretend you are going on a journey. You have only a knapsack. What items would you take?
2. What instructions would Jesus give if he were sending the apostles out today?
3. Share yours answers:
   As one of the apostles, I would find it hard to _____.
   One thing that prepares me to do God's work is _____.

DOING

1. As a family, have a summer Give-away Day. Go through the clothing and furnishings in your home. Strip yourselves of unnecessary belongings. Give them away. Resolve to live more simply. In the evening, have a special dessert to celebrate your new way of life.

2. Make your weekly scripture symbol—a knapsack. Place it in your home or on your SUNDAY THROUGHOUT THE YEAR banner.

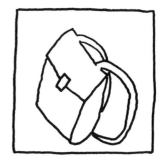

PRAYING

We go forth, Lord, to live a simple life. Possessing and taking care of too many things distracts us from you. We have little time left to spend with you and with others.

Help us to be eager to hear your call and to listen to your will. Send us wherever you wish. Ask of us whatever you desire. We depend only on you, Lord. We will take nothing but faith on our journey. Amen.

CYCLE B

16th Sunday of Ordinary Time (Mk 6:30-34)

REFLECTING

Yahweh is my shepherd.
I lack nothing.
In meadows of green grass he lets me lie.
To the waters of repose he leads me;
there he revives my soul.

— Psalm 23:1-2

Notice how sensitive Jesus is both to the needs of the apostles and to the needs of the people in today's gospel. The apostles had returned from preaching and healing. Separated from the presence of Jesus, tired and hungry from their journey, they needed to be alone with him. Jesus responded to their need. "You must come away to some lonely place all by yourselves and rest for a while."

But there were too many people around; this was not the place for rest. To find the lonely place, they set out in a boat.

But the needs of the people were great, too. They were like sheep without a shepherd; they had no one to lead them. They were weary and hungry for the words of Jesus. It was not difficult for many of them to determine where Jesus was going. They walked hurriedly around the Sea of Galilee and arrived before the boat. How surprised and disappointed the apostles must have been to see them! But Jesus pitied the people; he saw their deep hunger for instruction, for direction, for comfort. He began to teach them and his words filled their need.

TALKING

1. Is there a difference between wants and needs? What are some of the needs of your family? Talk about ways to satisfy these needs. How does Jesus answer your needs?

2. Share with your family the lonely place you go to rest. Talk about the need for rest in your life. How does prayer fit in with your need for rest?

3. Share your answers:
   Jesus invites me to ＿＿＿＿＿＿＿＿＿＿.
   The people needed ＿＿＿＿＿＿＿＿＿; the apostles needed
   ＿＿＿＿＿＿＿＿.
   These words of Jesus fill my being: ＿＿＿＿＿＿＿＿.

DOING

1. Pantomime this gospel scene. Then rest together while Psalm 23 is read.

2. Make your weekly scripture symbol—a sheep with the words "Come rest" written under it. Place it in your home or on your SUNDAY THROUGH-OUT THE YEAR banner.

PRAYING

Lord,
Like the apostles, we want to come and rest with you. We are weary and we long for your renewing presence.

Like the people, we are sometimes lost, sheep without a shepherd. We long for your word. We need you to give direction to our lives.

For satisfying all our needs, for the meadows of green grass and the waters of repose, we thank you, Lord. Amen.

Jul 18, 1982 / Jul 21, 1985 / Jul 17, 1988

17th Sunday of Ordinary Time (Jn 6:1-15)

REFLECTING

There was no rest for Jesus. Wherever he went, crowds followed. If he crossed a lake, the people ran around the lake to find him. If he went up the mountain, the crowds pursued him.

On this spring day men, women and children came to hear Jesus as he talked with his apostles on the hillside.

Jesus was sensitive not only to their spiritual hunger, but also to their physical need for nourishment. Turning to Philip, he asked where bread could be bought for the people. Philip was overwhelmed with the magnitude of the problem.

Andrew, the brother of Simon, told Jesus of a young boy with barley loaves and dried fish. Barley was the ordinary food of the poor. Jesus took the loaves of bread, gave thanks and passed the bread to the people. He did the same with the fish. How touching and beautiful is this scene!

We see that our Lord cares for us, gives us food to eat, and shows us how to give thanks to God for the gifts we have, for the very gift of life itself. Thank you, Jesus.

TALKING

1. Talk about the meaning of the Eucharist in your life. In what way do you think this miracle helped to prepare the people for the gift of Jesus in the Eucharist?

2. Consider the different people mentioned in this story: the young boy with the bread and fish, Philip, Andrew, the men, women and children. Which of these people would you have been most like? Why?

3. Share your answers:
   For spiritual growth, I hunger for _____.
   Seeing Jesus perform this miracle, I would have _____.
   I am most like Philip when I _____.

DOING

1. Jesus gave thanks to his Father before doing anything and in everything he did. Write and post a family litany of thanks. Add to this litany throughout the week.

2. Make your weekly scripture symbol—loaves and fish. Place it in your home or on your SUNDAY THROUGHOUT THE YEAR banner.

PRAYING

(Pray together before a meal. Stand with arms extended, palms upward.)

Leader: Lift up your hearts.
All: We lift them up to the Lord.
Leader: Let us give thanks to the Lord our God.
All: It is right to give him thanks and praise.
                              —from Eucharistic Prayer I

And we ask you to bless us, O Lord, and these your gifts which we are about to receive from your bounty, through Christ our Lord. Amen.

Jul 25, 1982 / Jul 28, 1985 / Jul 24, 1988

18th Sunday of Ordinary Time (Jn 6:24-35)

REFLECTING

In Charles Dickens' *Oliver Twist*, the young boy holds his empty bowl tightly as he extends it upward. With pleading eyes, and a faltering voice, he asks: "More, sir? May I have more food?"

Like Oliver, we plead with God for more. Unlike the cruel director of the orphanage, God continuously answers our needs as he has answered the needs of all his people throughout the ages.

After traveling only three days in the desert, the people grumbled against Moses and Aaron, complaining that they had no water to drink. Through Moses, God gave them water. In today's first reading (Ex 16:2-4,12-15), we hear of more bitter complaints against Moses and Aaron. This time the people had no food. Once again God gave prompt relief to their complaints. "Between the two evenings you shall eat meat, and in the morning you shall have bread to your heart's content."

The leaves of the tamarisk bush produce an excretion. It drops to the ground and becomes firm during the cool desert nights. Gathered before the sun meets it, this manna offers nourishment. Because of its sweet taste, the Bedouins even today consider this food a delicacy.

It was this manna from God that the people found in the morning. In the evening quail, tired from their migration southward, rested on the camp ground and became easy prey. The Israelites had enough to eat.

In today's gospel Jesus reveals himself as the Bread of Life:
"He who comes to me will never be hungry;
he who believes in me will never thirst."

TALKING

1. As a family, share the ways you express thanksgiving for Jesus, the Bread of Life. In what ways do you show gratitude for the life of each family member?

2. Talk about the desert experience of the Israelites. Recall times you have grumbled and complained when things have gone wrong. How do you handle the deserts of your own life?

3. Share your answers:
   Like Oliver, I need "more" _____.
   Jesus nourishes us _____.
   In thanksgiving for this gift of life from God, I say _____.

DOING

1. Bake bread and break it together at a family meal. Recall the many grains that made this loaf. Celebrate your oneness as a family.

2. Make your weekly scripture symbol—a loaf of bread. Place it in your home or on your SUNDAY THROUGHOUT THE YEAR banner.

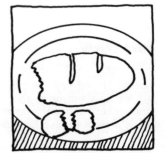

PRAYING

Response: The Lord gave them bread from heaven.
When the people in the desert were without food ...
When the 5,000 were hungry ...
When our ancestors longed for care and nourishment ...
When the world needed the gift of Jesus himself ...

Aug 1, 1982 / Aug 4, 1985 / Jul 31, 1988

19th Sunday of Ordinary Time (Jn 6:41-51)

REFLECTING

"Nobody knows the trouble I've seen
Nobody knows my sorrow
Nobody knows the troubles I've seen
Way beyond tomorrow."

—Negro spiritual

This lament of woe could easily have been on the lips of Elijah as he fled from the hands of the wicked Queen Jezebel and sought refuge in the desert. Physically, he was exhausted; spiritually, he was worn out, discouraged and afraid. He saw all his work as futile, having no meaning, no significance. We hear his despair in today's first reading (1 Kgs 19:4-8) as he prays to God: "I have had enough. Take my life ..."

God brings comfort to us in our moments of despair; he offered a scone baked on hot stones and a jar of water as comfort to Elijah. Twice, Elijah ate this nourishment. With this food, he received the strength to continue his journey to Mount Horeb where he was to experience the presence of God.

Like Elijah, we too become discouraged in our work, we lose heart, we experience futility. Our spirits become low. As God drew Elijah to himself, so he will draw each of us. His word will give us light for the journey; his food, the gift of his Son, the Bread of Life, will give us strength.

In today's gospel, Jesus asked for belief in him as the Son of God, as the living bread that comes down from heaven.

TALKING

1. Exhausted and discouraged, Elijah told God: "I have had enough." Talk about those moments in business, school and home life in which you felt the same way. How were you able to handle this discouragement? How do you find meaning in the work you do? Where do you turn to be renewed and strengthened? To whom?

2. Talk about the meaning of the Eucharist, the bread of life, in your daily life. How do you allow God to draw you to him? Talk about your belief in living forever through the Eucharist.

DOING

1. Make a collage of different occupations. Draw a path across the collage. On the path, write the words, "O, yes, Lord," as a sign of your hope that all people will allow God to draw them to himself for strength in the work they do.

2. Make your weekly scripture symbol—a jar of water and a scone. Place it in your home or on your SUNDAY THROUGHOUT THE YEAR banner.

PRAYING

(Say this prayer before family meals this week.)

God gave one house for all of us to dwell in.
It is called the world.
God distributed all things equally.
He kindled one sun for all:
stretched above us one roof, the sky;
and set one table, which is the earth.

But God gave us a much greater table than this.
It is the table of one loaf and one cup.

—St. John Chrysostom

Aug 8, 1982 / Aug 11, 1985 / Aug 7, 1988

CYCLE B

20th Sunday of Ordinary Time (Jn 6:51-58)

REFLECTING

> He who sings prays twice.

In music, we express our hearts. Like worship, music engages our whole person, calls for a total response from us. We may not want to be changed, we may not want to express deep inner feelings and thoughts, but music gives us little choice. It simply demands a response from us.

In our first reading (Eph 5:15-20), we discovered that the early Christian communities expressed themselves through psalms, hymns and inspired song. Filled with the Holy Spirit, they sang praise to God with all their hearts.

Through the 150 psalms of the Old Testament, people praise and worship God. Like all lyrical poetry, the psalms express our life, our laments, our joys, our sorrows, our need for forgiveness and protection. Each Sunday we praise God through the Responsorial Psalm during the Liturgy of the Word. Every day we have the opportunity to sing our praises to God through the psalms.

Through song we can celebrate and praise God and show gratitude for his presence among us. Song is a way to manifest our joy. What a glorious experience when the entire community gathered for prayer expresses its thanksgiving and joy in this way!

TALKING

1. Talk about the need for music in your life. With family members, share songs (popular and liturgical) which express for you your feelings of thanksgiving, hope, love, longing, joy.

2. How can you be alert to God's inspiration in the moments that you live? Prudence and right judgment are gifts of the Spirit. Talk about ways to open yourself to the life of the Spirit within you.

3. Share your answers:
   My favorite psalm is _____.
   In music I can express my _____.
   To live a life of prudence is to _____.

DOING

1. Have a family song fest. In round robin sing all the songs you know or have each family member begin a song, stopping at a chosen word. The next person must begin his or her song with that word.

2. Make your weekly scripture symbol—a musical note. Place it in your home or on your SUNDAY THROUGHOUT THE YEAR banner.

PRAYING

Lord,
We sing a new song to you.
We sing of joy and gladness,
We sing of praise and gratitude,
We sing of thanksgiving.
We sing our longings and dreams,
  our hopes, and promises.
Together as your people, we raise our voices in celebration of your life within us.
And we sing from our heart, from the deep innermost core of our being.
Our song is our prayer to you.

(Sing the Holy, Holy, Holy Lord from the Sunday Mass.)

Aug 18, 1985 / Aug 14, 1988

21st Sunday of Ordinary Time (Jn 6:59-69)

REFLECTING

We must make choices, choices similar to the one Joshua proposed to the people and the one Jesus offered the disciples. It was in faith that the people made their choice. It is in faith that we are called to make ours.

In our first reading (Jos 24:1-2a,15-17,18b) Joshua offers the 12 tribes this choice: Choose the Lord or choose the local gods. Without hesitation the people renew the covenant treaty. They acknowledge the Lord's role in their history, that it was the Lord who brought them out of slavery, protected them through the desert and gave them their new land. They promise to serve the Lord all their days.

In today's gospel Jesus stands before people who do not believe in him. He continues to offer his words as spirit and life, but because they do not have faith, the people turn and walk away.

As the people leave, Jesus turns to the apostles and asks the question that he asks each of us today: "What about you, do you want to go away too?" Peter immediately professed his faith: "Lord, who shall we go to? You have the message of eternal life, and we believe."

Every time we receive the Eucharist we are asked to profess our faith. It is through the Eucharist that we are made one, that we participate in the life of God himself. We will not go away. We will believe.

TALKING

1. Faith is a gift from the Father. How do you handle this gift? Do you put it away for safe-keeping? Use it daily? How do you welcome this gift and allow it to increase within you?

2. What words of Jesus are spirit and life for you? What words help you not only to see but understand? Like Peter and the apostles, reflect on your coming to know Jesus more and more.

3. Share your answers:
   I am like Peter because _____.
   I am like those who walked away because _____.

DOING

1. Write a covenant of faith with God and post your beliefs on a treaty. Like the people in the promised land, renew this covenant of faith daily during the week.

2. Make your weekly scripture symbol—a "YES/NO" sign. Place it in your home or on your SUNDAY THROUGHOUT THE YEAR banner.

PRAYING

Lord,
Your presence in the Eucharist overwhelms us! You continuously offer yourself to us. Where should we go without you? What would we be without you? It is only your words that give spirit and life, only your words that free us to say, "We will follow you; we will not go away."

Increase our faith. Ask your Father to grant that we may come to you. Let him draw us to you. Because we believe in you, we celebrate you! Amen.

Aug 22, 1982 / Aug 25, 1985 / Aug 21, 1988

CYCLE B

22nd Sunday of Ordinary Time (Mk 7:1-8a, 14-15, 21-23)

REFLECTING

Lord Jesus, Son of the living God, have mercy on me, a sinner.
—the Jesus Prayer

From the Eastern church comes the ancient practice of praying the Jesus Prayer. The 13 words of this prayer are repeated over and over again with interior reverence. This mantra (a prayer formula which is repeated monotonously) is done in rhythm with the breathing.

In today's gospel Jesus asks that we honestly appraise ourselves. What are our intentions in doing the things we do? Being aware of our weaknesses should not bring despondence; rather, we should feel grateful that God's pardon and mercy are ours if we but turn our hearts to him. The praying of the Jesus Prayer helps us to do this.

Our conduct must reflect what is in our hearts. James tells us in the second reading (Jas 1:17-18, 21b-22, 27) to humbly welcome the word that has already taken root in us. The implanted word has the power to save, to renew, to heal. We show welcome not only by reflecting on the presence of the word within us, by listening to the word in our heart, but by living the word through our actions.

We do God's word through the way we treat others. It is not enough simply to do no harm to others, we must actively help them. Do we feed the hungry, welcome the stranger, comfort the sorrowing? Do we counsel the doubtful, forgive all injuries, bear wrongs patiently? Do we tend the sick, visit those in prison, instruct the ignorant? By our actions, people shall come to know our hearts and the word that lives and grows within us.

TALKING

1. Consider the word of God already implanted in you. Share with the family the ways in which you are or could live that word.
2. Share your answers:
   For me, the Jesus Prayer is _____.
   I live God's word by _____.
   The one work of mercy I will do this week is _____.

DOING

1. Draw a fruit tree with roots on a large piece of cardboard. Cut pieces of fruit out of construction paper. Write the things you have done or will do for others on the fruit and place the fruit on the branches of the tree. Across the top of the tree, write "We live." By the roots, print "The word of God."

2. Make your weekly scripture symbol—a scroll with the words "Hear and do." Place it in your home or on your SUNDAY THROUGHOUT THE YEAR banner.

PRAYING

(Pray the Jesus Prayer, one of the following mantras or any phrase of your choice.)

Lord, I welcome your word.
My Lord and my God.
Jesus, I love you.
Into your hands, I give my spirit.
Lord, I turn to you. I love you.
Your word grows in me.

Aug 29, 1982 / Sep 1, 1985 / Aug 28, 1988

23rd Sunday of Ordinary Time (Mk 7:31-37)

REFLECTING

Sometimes we show the way we feel and the way we think through signs. In our culture a handshake says, "Good to see you, friend"; a smile says, "I like you"; a pat on the head says, "You are so good." Signs are a silent language; they convey messages to us.

Jesus used signs. He touched blind men; he blessed children; he laid hands on his friends, the apostles. Today, Jesus continues to act through signs, sacred signs called sacraments.

In today's gospel, Jesus used sacramental gestures, gestures which effect what they symbolize. He opened a deaf man's ears by placing his fingers into the man's ears; he loosened the man's tongue for clear speech by touching it with spittle. He sighed, looked up to heaven and spoke, "*Ephphatha*," which means "Be opened."

We should evaluate our attitudes toward others. How do we treat the handicapped, for example? Are we aware of the dignity and rights of each human person? Our second reading (Jas 2:1-5) reminds us to consider our attitude toward the rich, the successful, the educated, the socially prominent. Do we treat them with more respect than the poor, the handicapped, the unproductive, the downtrodden? With whom do we spend our time? Whom do we welcome into our homes?

TALKING

1. Talk about your attitude toward the handicapped. Become aware of what your community has done for them. What could you do as a family to preserve their rights and dignity as human persons?

2. Sacraments are sacred signs; they are actions of Jesus giving his Spirit to us. Talk about the seven sacraments and the gestures and words used in each. What does each sacrament do?

3. Share your answers:
   My ears are closed to Jesus' words when _____.
   I fail to speak clearly when _____.
   I need Jesus' word, "*Ephphatha*," in order to _____.

DOING

1. Post the words "See," "Hear," and "Speak" on the inside doors and mirrors of your home.

2. Make your weekly scripture symbol—the word "*Ephphatha*" in a conversation balloon. Place it in your home or on your SUNDAY THROUGHOUT THE YEAR banner.

PRAYING

Response: Amen.

May the eyes of the blind be opened ...
May the ears of the deaf be cleared ...
May the lame leap like a deer ...
May the tongues of the dumb sing for joy ...
(Lift your head and hands.)
May we treat all people with respect ...
May we preserve their dignity ...
May we guard their rights ...
May we serve and love others.

Sep 5, 1982 / Sep 8, 1985 / Sep 4, 1988

24th Sunday of Ordinary Time (Mk 8:27-35)

REFLECTING

How comforting it is to be with someone who is both generous and self-assured! We stand in awe of the confident way that person does things. With admiration and respect we relax in that person's presence and feel honored that we are a friend.

Perhaps this was the way Peter felt as he and the disciples walked through the villages watching Jesus cure the sick and heal the brokenhearted. Jesus was his hero. The hero asked Peter a simple question, "Who do you say I am?" Peter's answer: "You are the Christ." Then Jesus began to teach them that the Son of Man "was destined to suffer grievously, to be rejected ... and to be put to death, and after three days to rise again."

Peter was baffled. How could this happen to his hero? In his bewilderment, Peter tried to convince Jesus that all this was not necessary. Jesus' reply should also be our reply to temptation: "Get behind me, Satan!"

Jesus challenged his disciples, and he challenges us: "If anyone wants to be a follower of mine, let him renounce himself and take up his cross and follow me."

Was it any wonder that Peter wanted those steps not to be such difficult ones?

TALKING

1. Have each family member respond personally to Jesus' question: "Who do you say I am?"

2. How do you determine if the standards you live by are also God's standards? List and share these standards.

3. Share your answers:
   For me, a hero is _____.
   I find it difficult to follow Jesus in _____.
   If I were Peter, I would have _____.

DOING

1. To follow Jesus is to live his words, his life. Have a game challenge to recall through signs (your SUNDAY THROUGHOUT THE YEAR banner) what Jesus said and did. Take turns connecting the story with the sign until all the signs have been identified. Tally points for the right answers.

2. Make your weekly scripture symbol—a cross. Place it in your home or on your SUNDAY THROUGHOUT THE YEAR banner.

PRAYING

Lord,
You are the Christ! You are the hero! You freely chose to accept your cross and walk the path of suffering. Crosses are part of our human life. Crosses are problems and nobody likes them.

We cannot promise, Lord, that we will look forward to the crosses in our lives, but we promise that with your help and the help of our family we will try to carry them patiently when you do send them to us. Help us not to complain. Through our crosses, help us find a way to forget ourselves and walk in your footsteps. Amen.

25th Sunday of Ordinary Time (Mk 9:30-37)

REFLECTING

There are people in our lives who bring forth the child that is deep within each of us. In today's gospel, Jesus welcomes a child. The child welcomes him. No one is threatened or defensive in this relationship.

How happy and peace-filled our lives would be if we would allow God to put his arms around us as a father does his child! But it is hard for us to be dependent upon someone, to give up self-reliance and to cast all our cares upon God.

There are so many subtle forms of ambition. Sometimes we want to be first even at the expense of others. In these moments we seek glory and fame just for ourselves.

It was only human for the apostles to be ambitious and to ask, "Who is the most important among us?" The answer can only be that we are all important; we are children of God.

TALKING

1. List the qualities of a child. Which of these qualities are still alive in you? How do you call forth and welcome the child in others?
2. Talk about the subtle forms of ambition, of wanting to be first even at the expense of others.
3. Share your answers:
   The thing I want to do most in my life is _____.
   People threaten others by their _____.

DOING

1. Make a series of attached paper doll cutouts. Have family members write their names on them. Display the cutouts on the refrigerator door with the words: "God is our Father."
2. Make your weekly scripture symbol—a paper cutout of a child. Place it in your home or on your SUNDAY THROUGHOUT THE YEAR banner.

PRAYING

It is so hard, Lord, so hard to welcome you as a servant. But we know that in welcoming you, we meet God who sent you. We are only important because you have made us your children. Let us never seek glory for ourselves but simply reflect your wonder and beauty in what we do. Help the child to shine forth in our parents and our brother(s) and sister(s) and in ourselves. Amen.

(As children of God, hold hands and pray the Our Father.)

Sep 19, 1982 / Sep 22, 1985 / Sep 18, 1988

26th Sunday of Ordinary Time (Mk 9:38-43, 45, 47-48)

REFLECTING

God uses a cloud in the Old and New Testament as a sign of his protection. As in today's first reading (Nm 11:25-29), there are many instances in the bible in which Yahweh appeared or spoke in a cloud. Do you remember the cloud in the baptism of Jesus and at the transfiguration, and the cloud that led the Chosen People across the desert? For Moses the cloud was a sign of God's presence.

Moses was a great leader and prophet, a man filled with the Spirit. One day God gave this same Spirit to 70 other people in the camp. While Moses rejoiced in this sharing of the Spirit, his friend and aide, Joshua, feared that Moses would lose his power as God's spokesman.

Moses' response is beautiful. He *rejoices!* He is not jealous that others are chosen as a channel of God's Spirit. His desire is that all people receive the same gift of the Spirit.

It is good for us to remember what jealousy can do to family living. We have only to think of Cain and Abel, Joseph and his brothers, Saul and David. Perhaps we should examine our own feelings toward friends or family members. We are not rivals but, like Moses, we rejoice as the Spirit works through all people.

Clouds cover the entire earth. Just as no one owns the clouds, so no one can claim the exclusive possession of God or his Spirit. The Spirit of God lives in all who love God and do his work.

TALKING

1. Have family members share three things (gifts) that they do best.

2. Talk about the different people in your life who let the Spirit of God speak and act through them.

3. Share your answers:
   Like Joshua, I feel jealous and envious when _____.
   I rejoice that the Spirit has given me the gift of _____ and to
   (*Name*) the gift of _____.

DOING

1. Lie outside on your back and watch the movement of the clouds. Remember the cloud as a sign of the presence of God in your life.

2. Make your weekly scripture symbol—a cloud. Place it in your home or on your SUNDAY THROUGHOUT THE YEAR banner.

PRAYING

(Marshmallows remind us of clouds. Place a bowl of marshmallows on your table.)

Response: Forgive us, Lord.
For the times we are jealous of what others can do . . .
For the times we are envious of what others have . . .
For the times we are protective of what we can do . . .
For the times we are selfish with what we have . . .

Like Moses, Lord, let us rejoice in the gifts of others. Help us to celebrate ourselves as gifts. Make us a channel, Lord, an instrument of your will as we use our gifts for others. Renew us daily in the life of your Spirit. Together, let us celebrate clouds as a sign of your presence and protection. Amen.

(Family members eat the marshmallows.)

Sep 26, 1982 / Sep 29, 1985 / Sep 25, 1988

27th Sunday of Ordinary Time (Mk 10:2-16)

REFLECTING

Have you ever felt alone? Have you walked through your home and found only silence? Have you ever been in school, or on the playground, or in your backyard when no one was there?

Today's first reading (Gn 2:18-24) tells us about a day, long ago. God looked over the world he had made and said, "It is not good that the man should be alone. I will make him a helpmate." And woman was created. Man and woman were united and bound together in an intimate friendship with one another and with God. Man was no longer alone.

Marriage is a covenant, a friendship pact, a call to live together in love. Love overcomes loneliness.

Love causes oneness. Not only are a man and woman in marriage responsible for each other and their children, but the children are responsible in love for each other and for their parents. May we remember always the covenant between God and his people, the covenant between a man and a woman, and the covenant between children and their parents.

TALKING

1. Talk about the difference between being alone and being lonely. Name situations in which you have felt lonely. How did you handle the feeling?

2. In the covenant God offers a friendship pact to his people. Talk about the way you live this covenant as a parent or a child.

3. Share your answers:
   With my family, I enjoy _____.
   When I am lonely I _____.
   I show my love for my family by _____.

DOING

1. Write and post a statement (covenant) of your family love. Have each family member sign this covenant. Draw a sign of your oneness on this proclamation.

2. Make your weekly scripture symbol—a ring. Place it in your home or on your SUNDAY THROUGHOUT THE YEAR banner.

PRAYING

(Before God, recite this family promise. The leader reads a line and family members repeat it.)

We (*each person says his or her name*) accept family life.
We promise to be with one another in good and bad times.
We promise to be faithful.
We promise to love and to forgive.
We promise to be patient.
We promise to welcome Jesus as a friend into our family life.
We promise to honor one another all the days of our life.

In the name of the Father, and of the Son, and of the Holy Spirit. Amen.

CYCLE B

Oct 3, 1982 / Oct 6, 1985 / Oct 2, 1988

28th Sunday of Ordinary Time (Mk 10:17-30)

REFLECTING

Mike ran excitedly to the Tiger Paws Club House door. "Can I join? I know all your rules." He became sad and left when he was told that to join he must share his baseball card collection.

Sometimes we are like this young boy. We are excited with the Good News Jesus preached but find the full demands of his words difficult. Like the man in today's gospel, we run to Jesus, kneel before him and ask what we should do to share in a life that will go on forever. When Jesus discovered that the man had been living a good life already, he looked at him with love. This *look* spoke of warmth, approval and acceptance. How we long for this same look!

But this look also spoke of the full demands of discipleship: "Go and sell everything you own and give the money to the poor and you will have treasure in heaven; then come, follow me." Like the man, we are asked to give up everything to follow Jesus.

"It is easier for a camel to pass through the eye of a needle than for a rich man to enter the kingdom of God," Jesus says. Could it be that riches distract us from God? Could it be that riches are too time-consuming to gather and to keep? Or do we become too attached to them? Consumed by them?

How surprised the disciples of Jesus must have been to hear their concept of wealth as a sign of God's blessing turned upside down. To be his followers we are asked to give up everything that turns us away from God. Our reward will be the blessing of God's creation in which we daily live, along with his look of love—and eternal life.

TALKING

1. Name things you own or do that could distract you from God. How can we give up everything to follow Jesus?

2. Why is it hard for a rich person to enter the kingdom of God? Share your thoughts on Jesus' meaning of being rich.

3. Share your answers:
   For me, money is _____.
   To follow Jesus, I will _____.
   The blessings of God in creation are clear to me in _____.

DOING

1. Gather fall leaves as a reminder of the blessing and beauty of God's creation. Have a fall house-cleaning of things you do not need. Share these things with others.

2. Make your weekly scripture symbol—a dollar sign. Place it in your home or on your SUNDAY THROUGHOUT THE YEAR banner.

PRAYING

Lord,
It is sometimes hard to follow you. Help us to see you in the people we meet and in the things we do. Help us to live a simple life. Give us the strength to set aside anything that turns us from you. To possess things does not mean to be possessed by them. To live *in* this world is not to be *of* this world.

Your demands, Jesus, are hard to follow in our world. But your look of love helps us to remember. Your look of love gives us the courage to live those demands daily. Amen.

Oct 10, 1982 / Oct 13, 1985 / Oct 9, 1988

29th Sunday of Ordinary Time (Mk 10:35-45)

REFLECTING

> The poor have helped us to learn something beautiful. They have taught us their love for one another. Each one does what he or she can. We don't have to think of numbers. We can love one person at a time, serve one person at a time.
>
> —Mother Teresa of Calcutta

In today's gospel, Jesus is called teacher. As teacher, he shares with us an important lesson: We are to serve others and not be served. Jesus not only taught this lesson, he lived it. He became a servant, he even accepted death for the wrongs of all people.

There is a paradox here. Our God, mighty and strong, is a servant. He asks not that we serve him but that we allow him to serve us. How extraordinary is our God! Like Mother Teresa, our greatness consists in being called to be a servant also.

Our role as servant could overwhelm us. In living a life of service to others, Mother Teresa offers us sage advice. Simply love and serve one person at a time. And we do this one day at a time.

TALKING

1. Talk about Mother Teresa and the way in which she serves.

2. List the occupations in which people serve others. Do you think it is easier to serve or to be served? Does the Christian concept of service run counter to our culture?

3. Share your answers:
   This week I will serve others by _____.
   For me, Mother Teresa of India is _____.

DOING

1. Make and post a document with the words "I have come to serve" in bold letters across the top. Have each family member sign this document.

2. Make your weekly scripture symbol—a small scroll with the words "I have come to serve" on it. Place it in your home or on your SUNDAY THROUGHOUT THE YEAR banner.

PRAYING

Response: I have come to serve.
For the poor who have no food ...
For the sad who have lost heart ...
For the lonely who have no friends ...
For the sick who have no hope ...
For those who have forgotten to love themselves ...

Help us, Jesus, to understand the way you call each of us to serve. Give us the courage to serve in a world that ridicules the server. Together as a family, may we become like you, a servant to all. Amen.

CYCLE B

30th Sunday of Ordinary Time (Mk 10:46-52)

REFLECTING

A reddish-brown and gold leaf drifted gently in the breeze. Slowly, it fell to the ground. Three-year-old Lisa ran excitedly to pick up the leaf. "Mommy, look," she cried, "God has been painting again!"

Like the other seasons, the fall offers us the opportunity to look and to see. When we *look*, we know only that summer is ending and winter will soon begin. When we *see*, we have the eyes of the child and rejoice in the gift of God's creation.

Jesus walked and talked with many people. Some people looked at him and saw only the carpenter's son who had become a teacher. Others did more than just look. Through faith they *saw* God's Son.

One day Jesus was teaching as he walked along the Jericho road. A blind beggar named Bartimaeus called out, "Son of David, Jesus, have pity on me." He kept shouting this messianic title until he was noticed. Jesus asked him, "What do you want me to do for you?" "Master," the beggar said, "let me see again." In his calm, caring way, Jesus replied, "Go; your faith has saved you."

The blind beggar asked to be healed. Jesus offers his healing to all, yet sometimes we do not ask. We forget to ask Jesus for anything, to reach out, to cry out for his healing presence which is always there.

Through deep faith this man *saw* Jesus as the Son of God; he saw more than some of the disciples saw. The eyes of faith see that which cannot be seen and understand that which cannot be understood. In faith, let us see and ask to be healed.

TALKING

1. Talk about the meaning of faith in your life. Does faith help you see better? How do you renew your faith daily?
2. Share your answers:
   Like Bartimaeus, I would ask this of Jesus: _____.
   To really *see* another is _____.

DOING

1. Sometimes we are blind to the goodness in others and the goodness in ourselves. Make a poster with words "Of thee I sing" across the top. Place all your family names of the poster and throughout the week write affirming words or draw signs of good things you see each person do under his or her name.

2. Make your weekly scripture symbol—the word "See." Place it in your home or on your SUNDAY THROUGHOUT THE YEAR banner.

PRAYING

(As a sign of your faith, stand for this creed.)
Through faith, Lord,
We believe in God who made this wonderful world.
We believe in the Spirit who keeps this world going through so much love.
We believe in Jesus who became like us so we would become like him.
We believe that life is so important it will go on forever.
We believe in all the people that have been made, that together with God we can laugh and love forever. Amen.

31st Sunday of Ordinary Time (Mk 12:28b-34)

REFLECTING

During our school days, we meet new teachers who ask us to follow their instructions.

Long ago, the people met God through Moses. God asked the people to follow Moses' instructions in order to become totally dedicated to him and to worship him alone. The people of the New Testament meet God through Jesus who is the new teacher of God's law.

In today's gospel a scribe asks the question that people of all times have asked and discussed: What is the most important commandment? Jesus says: "You must love the Lord your God with all your heart, with all your soul, with all your mind, and with all your strength. You must love your neighbor as yourself." The rest of the Law flows from this double commandment. The scribe nods his head in agreement; so do we.

TALKING

1. Talk about ways to remember to love God with your whole heart, soul, mind and strength. List ways to show your love for your neighbor.

2. When you do wrong, you turn away from God. When your relationship with God is poor, you endanger your relationship with yourself and others. Talk about ways you can re-establish your relationship with God, self and others.

3. Share your answers:
   To remember to love God with all my heart, I _____.
   As a family this week, we can show our love to one another by _____.

DOING

1. The Shema, which was written on a rolled scroll, was Israel's daily prayer to God. Write the words of the two great commandments on a scroll (see Reflecting). Open and read from the scroll as a family prayer to begin each day of this week.

2. Make your weekly scripture symbol—two overlapping hearts. Place it in your home or on your SUNDAY THROUGHOUT THE YEAR banner.

PRAYING

God,
You have called us to be your people. You have asked that we choose you as our God. You have asked that we love you with all our heart, soul, mind and strength. It is so easy to forget you in our busy world, to turn away from you. Help us to know your presence, to see your love. You will know that we love you through the way we love our neighbor as ourself.

We love you, God. Amen.

32nd Sunday of Ordinary Time (Mk 12:38-44)

REFLECTING

Cesar Chavez ... Archbishop Helder Camara ... Sr. Maria Iglesias ... Mother Teresa—
these men and women have been called and have chosen to work with the poor of our
world. In Latin America, Upper Volta, India, Appalachia, with the migrant worker, the
American Indian, the elderly—these are some of the places and people that need our
time, our energy and our money.

Today's gospel tells us both how to live and how not to live a Christian life. There are
two choices:

Choice no. 1—Be like the scribe. Make possessions all-important. Take from the poor
and weak. Work only for recognition. Try to be noticed. Parade in your finest clothes
and speak loudly of your accomplishments. Be kind and giving only when people can
see you.

Choice no. 2—Be like the widow. Be devoted to God. Give of yourself to others. Be
generous. Help those who have been hurt by others. Walk in the shoes of another.
Experience with empathy their needs, and then reach out and answer those needs. In
humility, love God and with generosity, love your neighbor.

TALKING

1. Talk about the Third World. What responsibility do you have to the poor?

2. Discuss the two options for living. Give examples of these options chosen and lived
in the world today.

3. Share your answers:
   As a family, we show our responsibility to the poor by _____.
   In Choice No. 1, I find myself wanting to _____.
   In Choice No. 2, I find it hard to _____.

DOING

1. Make a container for the kitchen table. Collect
money for the poor.

2. Make your weekly scripture symbol—two small
coins. Place it in your home or on your SUNDAY
THROUGHOUT THE YEAR banner.

PRAYING

(Slowly read the Responsorial Psalm from today's Mass.
Pause and reflect after each statement.)

Response: Praise the Lord, my soul!
Lord, forever, faithful,
gives justice to those denied it,
gives food to the hungry,
gives liberty to prisoners ...

The Lord restores sight to the blind,
the Lord straightens the bent,
the Lord protects the stranger,
he keeps the orphan and widow ...

The Lord loves the virtuous,
and frustrates the wicked.
The Lord reigns for ever,
your God, Zion, from age to age ...

Nov 7, 1982 / Nov 10, 1985 / Nov 6, 1988

33rd Sunday of Ordinary Time (Mk 13:24-32)

REFLECTING

There is a chill in the air. The trees have lost their leaves. There is a quietness in the earth. There are signs that tell us that winter will soon be here.

Signs are important to us. A hand placed on the head of a child, a listening alertness to the concerns of another, a note of encouragement left on a pillow or in a lunch bag, these signs speak of our love and of God's presence in that love.

In today's gospel Jesus asks us to learn a lesson from the fig tree. When we see the sprouting leaves of the fig tree, we know that summer is approaching. There are also signs by which we will know and recognize that Christ is coming to gather all his people to himself.

We are told to be watchful for the day of Christ's coming. Be prepared. There is no need to fear his return as long as we live the Good News faithfully each day. Though we know not the hour, we are confident that we will see together the glory and splendor of God our Father.

TALKING

1. Signs are important in life. Talk about the signs which speak of home, school, business, the seasons. Why should you not be worried when you see the signs for the end, the Second Coming of Jesus?

2. Share your answers:
   I show my love for my family by _____.
   In our home, the sign of _____ reminds me of God's presence.
   When I see _____ I turn to God and talk with him.

DOING

1. Draw the outline of a fig tree. Cut out leaves separately. Have family members write their names on the leaves and paste them on the tree as a sign of preparing for the Second Coming of Christ.

2. Make your weekly scripture symbol—an outline of a fig tree with sprouting leaves. Place it in your home or on your SUNDAY THROUGHOUT THE YEAR banner.

PRAYING

Response: Keep us safe, God. You are our hope.
When we feel troubled and disturbed ...
When we feel lost and frightened ...
When we feel alone and abandoned ...

Give us signs, Lord, signs of your love for us, signs of your presence with us. Help us to always be prepared to welcome you into our hearts at any time and in any place. As a family we long for your coming. Amen.

CYCLE B

Solemnity of Christ the King (Jn 18:33b-37)

REFLECTING

"I'm not kidding. I really did see Miguel pass our house on his bike," explains Bernie with crossed fingers.

"Hey, crosses aren't allowed, you have to tell the truth," replies Bernie's younger brother.

As children we sometimes played the game of crossing our fingers when we were exaggerating or not telling the truth. In today's gospel we discover the importance of telling, listening and understanding the truth.

Pilate asked Jesus if he were a king. Jesus' answer defined a king not in political terms as a monarch reigning in power in a particular land, but in prophetic terms as a ruler reigning in truth in the hearts of all people.

If we belong to the truth we will understand the sense in which Jesus has a kingdom and is a king. Pilate did not understand or live the truth. Even though he declared Jesus not guilty, he still allowed him to be crucified.

How often we evade the truth! We may use I.D. cards that do not bear our name, change price tags, take advantage of the mistakes that others make. We may exaggerate, rationalize or even lie to make ourselves look important.

Let us listen to the truth even when we don't want to hear it and speak the truth even when it is inconvenient. "I came into the world for this: to bear witness to the truth; and all who are on the side of truth listen to my voice."

TALKING

1. Compare the type of king the people wanted after Jesus multiplied the loaves and fishes (Jn 6:15) to the king that Jesus reveals he is in today's gospel.

2. Talk about truth. What are some ways people choose to evade the truth? What helps do you use for speaking and living the truth?

3. Share your answers:
   For me, lying is _____.
   I am most like Pilate when I _____.

DOING

1. Write a proclamation of truth. Have family members sign this declaration to show their acceptance of Jesus as king. Make a three-dimensional crown and small triangular flags to use in a procession (see Praying, below). After the procession use the crown as a table centerpiece for the week, post the proclamation, and put the flags on the doors of your home.

2. Make your weekly scripture symbol—a crown. Place it in your home or on your SUNDAY THROUGHOUT THE YEAR banner.

PRAYING

Dear Jesus,
You are king! You have come into our lives to reveal your Father. You have come to help us believe in him and to love all people with him.
We hear your voice only when we live in truth. Help us to celebrate you as king, to shout your praises, and to glorify your reign forever in our hearts. Amen.

(With ceremony and song, process around your home with the crown, the proclamation and the flags.)

Nov 21, 1982 / Nov 24, 1985 / Nov 20, 1988

CYCLE C

SUNDAY THROUGHOUT THE YEAR Banner—Cycle C

1st Sunday of Advent (Lk 21:25-28, 34-36)

REFLECTING

We prepare and wait for the coming of Jesus. As a family we stand with head high, confident, persevering and prayerful. We try to live in hope and peace, to enjoy God's life in the present as we wait for the fullness of his promise in the future. As we watch for Jesus' coming, we try to live our lives without being too involved in the things of the world. We pray daily. We stand secure before the Lord.

Though many contemporaries of Jesus believed that the Second Coming would be in their lifetime, Luke, our primary evangelist for this C cycle, was convinced that this coming would be delayed until *all* people had heard the gospel. We are called to help others in this hearing.

We await the Second Coming just as the people awaited the birth of Jesus 2,000 years ago. Though these comings represent a past and future, there is also the daily coming of Jesus. In all of his comings, may we welcome him.

TALKING

1. *Advent* means "coming." Talk about the different ways Jesus comes to us.
2. How can we live *in* this world and yet not be *of* this world? In what ways should we be on watch as we await the Second Coming?
3. Share your answers:
   For me, Advent is _____.
   My favorite family prayer is _____.
   As a family, during Advent we will _____.

DOING

1. Make a Jesse tree on paper (like a family tree) or from a real branch. Make signs for three people who waited for the coming of Jesus: Noah (an ark), Abraham (a tent), Isaiah (a scroll). Consider the way each of these people prepared for the coming of Jesus. Throughout Advent, signs of different people will be added to the Jesse tree (see praying).

2. Make your weekly scripture symbol—a "Be on watch" sign. Place it in your home or on your SUNDAY THROUGHOUT THE YEAR banner.

PRAYING

You are coming, Lord Jesus!

We feel joy and excitement as we prepare together for your coming. Help us to make a gift of ourselves, knowing always that,

> "What we are is your gift to us,
> What we become is our gift to you."

Thank you for the gift of Noah, Abraham, Isaiah.

(Place the signs of these people on the Jesse tree.)

May we help others to become a gift. Amen.

CYCLE C

Nov 28, 1982 / Dec 1, 1985 / Nov 27, 1988

2nd Sunday of Advent (Lk 3:1-6)

REFLECTING

Like a troubadour of old, a solitary voice sings of our need for repentance and belief in the good news of Jesus. John the Baptist calls every nation and all people to change their ways, to repent in preparation for the coming of Jesus.

John is not the Messiah; he is not like the prophet Elijah or Moses. He is a voice. When we hear this voice, we know that we must make straight the way of the Lord. Like the prophet Isaiah, John has been called by God to show us the road that will take us home to God, the road that will lead us to experience God in our daily lives.

As Christian families we are called to become signs of hope to one another and signs of forgiveness for one another. Just as we prepare our home for Christians with decorations and gifts, so we prepare ourselves inside for Christ's coming. Together we live at home with God.

TALKING

1. Recall and share all you know about the life of John the Baptist.
2. December 8 is the feast of the Immaculate Conception. How did Mary help prepare the way of the Lord? What are some ways we can "make ready the way of the Lord"?
3. Share your answers:
   What interests me most about John the Baptist is _____.
   As a voice, my message would be _____.

DOING

1. Make signs for these Old Testament figures: Ruth (a bundle of wheat), Jeremiah (a clay pot), John (the word "John"). Consider the way each of these people prepared for the coming of Jesus. Be prepared to place these signs on the Jesse tree during Praying.
2. Make your weekly scripture symbol—a banner on a stick with the word "Prepare." Place it in your home or on your SUNDAY THROUGHOUT THE YEAR banner.

PRAYING

(Hang the signs you made in Doing #1 on the Jesse tree.)
God,
Help us to become like John the Baptist and prepare the way of the Lord. May we begin to think and love like Jesus and show kindness even to the people we may not like. Give us sensitive eyes to see the poor and sad, the lonely and hurting, and give us helping hands to reach out and heal.

If we prepare as John did, then we will have great joy at Christmas when Jesus comes into our lives in a special way. Amen.

3rd Sunday of Advent (Lk 3:10-18)

REFLECTING

Did you ever wait for someone to call?
Did you ever wait to meet someone?
Did you ever wait for Christmas or your birthday or a picnic?
Did you ever wait for spring to come?
Hope is *waiting* for a good thing to happen.

We wait for babies to be born.
We wait for people to love us as much as we love them.
We wait for peace and joy and understanding.
Some people waited thousands of years for one man to come.
Hope is *waiting together* for a good thing to happen.

Sometimes it's hard to wait. We get tired; we become discouraged or sad; sometimes we even cry. It seems that our winter will never end. Then, all of a sudden and—quickly, gently, from deep inside—we remember who we are and why we are, and we know that our spring will come again. We remember that Jesus will come again.

Hope is *waiting together a long, long time* for a good thing to happen.

We have waited together a long, long time for Jesus to come. Paul tells us in the second reading (Phil 4:4-7) to rejoice for the Lord is near. May we rejoice together for a good thing that is to happen, the birth of Jesus.

TALKING

1. Talk about the different times you have waited for good things to happen. Is it harder to wait alone or with friends?

2. Share your answers:
   It is hard to wait for _____.
   While I wait, I _____.
   One time I experienced hope was _____.

DOING

1. For your Jesse tree, make signs for Joseph (a cloud), Moses (tablet of laws) and Deborah (justice scales.) Consider the way each of these people prepared for the coming of Jesus. Be prepared to place these signs on the Jesse tree during Praying.

2. Make your weekly scripture symbol—a pennant. Write "Rejoice" on the pennant. Place it in your home or on your SUNDAY THROUGHOUT THE YEAR banner.

PRAYING

Lord,
We rejoice as we wait together for a good thing to happen. We rejoice that you have called us as a family to prepare for your coming into our hearts at Christmas. We rejoice in your gift of hope for a new world. We rejoice in Moses, Deborah, Joseph, and all the men and women who waited thousands of years for one man to come.

(Place the signs on the Jesse tree.)

Bless us, O Lord, for the gift which we are about to receive, the one for whom we have been preparing. Amen.

Dec 12, 1982 / Dec 15, 1985 / Dec 11, 1988

4th Sunday of Advent (Lk 1:39-45)

REFLECTING

"Welcome. Come in. It is so good to see you again. I'm thrilled you came."

How happy we are when someone comes to visit, particularly someone whom we care deeply about. And how welcome the visitor feels when greeted with warmth and enthusiasm.

Mary was touched by the presence of God in a special way. She trusted the presence. In this presence, she reached out to answer the needs of others. What a beautiful family scene—one cousin going to help another!

Elizabeth greeted Mary with a blessing, a blessing of honor and respect, a blessing of joy and thanksgiving that the mother of the Lord should come to visit her.

How surprised Mary was when she discovered that her cousin Elizabeth already knew her secret. Her response was to praise God for his goodness. Like Mary, let us look at the gifts God has given us and then use these gifts for others. Like Mary, let us hear the word of God and be eager to live that Word. Let us live in gratitude and thanksgiving for the presence of God in our world.

TALKING

1. Discuss the joyful events in Mary's life—and in yours. Share family stories of the preparation for the birth or adoption of each child. With whom was the news that a child was expected first shared?

2. Recall visits the family has made to relatives or friends. Talk about these experiences. Plan to visit someone you have not seen in a long time.

3. Share your answers:
    To help a family member, I will _____.
    My blessing to Mary is _____.
    I praise God for his goodness by _____.

DOING

1. For your Jesse tree, make signs for David (a crown), Jonah (a whale) and Mary (a heart). Consider the way each of these people prepared for the coming of Jesus. Be ready to place signs on the Jesse tree during Praying.

2. Make your weekly scripture symbol—a sign of greeting hands. Place it in your home or on your SUNDAY THROUGHOUT THE YEAR banner.

PRAYING

(Pray the Angelus as a family.)

The Angel of the Lord declared unto Mary
And she was conceived by the Holy Spirit.
Hail, Mary, full of grace . . .
Behold the handmaid of the Lord
Be it done unto me according to your Word.
Hail Mary, full of grace . . .
And the Word was made flesh
And dwelled among us.
Hail Mary, full of grace . . .
Pray for us, O Holy Mother of God
That we may be made worthy of the promises of Christ.

(Place the signs of David, Jonah and Mary on the Jesse tree.)

Dec 19, 1982 / Dec 22, 1985 / Dec 18, 1988

Feast of the Holy Family (Lk 2:41-52)

REFLECTING

In today's second reading (Col 3:12-21), Paul tells us that because we are holy, beloved, and God's chosen ones—his family—we are to wear the new garments of Christ. We are to clothe ourselves with these five virtues: compassion, humility, meekness, patience and forgiveness. When we live these virtues, we imitate Christ. When we live these virtues, we free ourselves and those around us to live and respond fully to God's call.

Family life should build up the spirit of the members for when one loses heart, when one becomes discouraged, the spirit is crushed.

The basic attitude that we have toward life is reflected in our family living. We express Christ's work in us through peace, thankfulness and joyful song. In this type of family Jesus grew in wisdom and years. In their home at Nazareth, Mary, Joseph and Jesus worked and prayed together; they supported, comforted and helped one another. Together they found meaning in the relationships among family members just as we do today.

Let us pray that we will continue to grow as a family through love and hardship, through joy and misunderstandings, through striving and caring.

TALKING

1. Share with family members moments of frustration and discouragement because of what someone said or did to you. How do you handle these moments? Talk about ways to build up the spirit of one another.
2. Share your answers:
   The family duty I most enjoy is _____.
   My spirit is built up when _____.
   Our family is like the Holy Family when _____.

DOING

1. As a family, plan an hour of working together, an hour of praying together and an hour of playing together this week.
2. Make your weekly scripture symbol—a house. Write in the name of each family member. Place it in your home or on your SUNDAY THROUGHOUT THE YEAR banner.

PRAYING

Eternal Father,
We want to live as Jesus, Mary and Joseph,
in peace with you and one another. . . .
Grant this through Christ our Lord. Amen.

—from the Prayer after Communion
of the Mass of the Holy Family

CYCLE C

Dec 26, 1982/Dec 29, 1985

Feast of the Baptism of the Lord (Lk 3:15-16, 21-22)

REFLECTING

All of us want to know if the work we do is worthwhile and benefits others. Sometimes we wonder if we should be doing something else with our lives. How comforting it would be if a visible stamp of approval could be placed upon our work.

Jesus received the approval of his Father after his baptism. The Holy Spirit descended on him like a dove and a voice was heard: "You are my Son, the Beloved; my favor rests on you." With this official stamp of approval, Jesus received the Spirit. He is the new Israel upon whom God's Spirit rests.

With the Spirit, Jesus began his mission. Luke consistently shows the Holy Spirit directing the work of Jesus. At our baptism, the Holy Spirit comes to each of us. Our confirmation, our new Pentecost, marks and seals this relationship with the Spirit.

In today's gospel, we see Jesus praying. Before important decisions and moments in his life, Luke revealed Jesus in prayer: before teaching, before choosing the apostles, before healing, before a difficult undertaking, before beginning his public ministry. Jesus allowed the Spirit within to give focus to his prayer life. He prayed out of his awareness of God and of himself.

Through our baptism, we are turned toward God. We have a mission, a mission to tell others of the way God has touched us, a mission to share with others the blessings we have received. With the Spirit present in all that we do, we begin. We walk the road marked by Jesus. Together as God's family, brothers and sisters to one another, we walk in his favor. We are stamped with his approval.

TALKING

1. Talk about the need for prayer in your life. When, where and with whom do you pray? Share with family members the prayer you say before making an important decision.

2. Through baptism, you receive the gift of the Spirit. At confirmation you are strengthened and sealed in the Spirit. Share signs of the presence of the Spirit in your family life.

3. Share your answers:
   I know God's presence when I _____.
   For me, prayer is_____.

DOING

1. Design and post on the refrigerator door a "stamp of approval" for your family. Have family members place their names under the stamp.

2. Make your weekly scripture symbol—a sign of water. Place it in your home or on your SUNDAY THROUGHOUT THE YEAR banner.

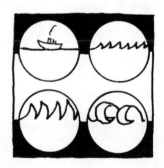

PRAYING

God, our Father,
Stamp us with your approval for the work you have chosen us to do. Be well pleased as we try to live our lives for you. You have showed us your favor by giving us your Spirit through baptism. The Spirit is now present in all that we do.

Help us to hear your voice as Jesus did. Speak with us. Speak through others to us. And as we listen, please give direction to the work we are doing, and the confidence in ourselves to do that work. Amen.

(Bless the family members with water to show God's approval of the work they do.)

Jan 9, 1983 / Jan 12, 1986

2nd Sunday of Ordinary Time (Jn 2:1-12)

REFLECTING

One day, the gospel tells us, Jesus and his friends gathered for a wedding party. Mary was present, too. There was laughter and rejoicing. In those days, a marriage celebration sometimes lasted many days. It is no wonder they ran out of wine.

Mary, with her deep concern for the needs of others, became aware that there was no more wine. Though his "hour has not come yet," Jesus, with deep respect for his mother and friends, performs his first public miracle by changing six jars of water into wine.

By attending this marriage celebration, Jesus not only tells us something about himself as a young man, but by his presence gives a blessing to marriage. In this miracle, we have a glimpse into kingdom life, a glimpse of Jesus' glory, a glimpse of the power of the one who sent Jesus to us, his Father.

The water that is made into wine is a sign of the new life of the Christian community, the new life of gladness and joy. Let us live in this joy as people of the kingdom.

TALKING

1. In what way does the wedding feast of Cana reveal Jesus to us? Make this Cana wedding feast come alive by picturing the day's festivities in your mind and then talking about the different things that happened or could have happened. This is a good way to begin to pray about an event in the life of Jesus. Share your thoughts with one another.

2. Talk about the different meals Jesus ate with his friends. How does a meal or celebration bring you closer to one another? Recall a celebration that did this for you.

3. Share your answers:
When I celebrate with my friends, I _____.
I am filled with joy and gladness when _____.
To see water changed into wine, I _____.

DOING

1. Plan a family party with food, song and decorations to experience the closeness of community that a celebration brings.

2. Make your weekly scripture symbol—a jar. Place it in your home or on your SUNDAY THROUGHOUT THE YEAR banner.

PRAYING

(Extend your hands for this blessing.)

Response: Amen.

May Jesus who was present at the wedding in Cana bless us and our families
and friends . . .
May we all be blessed and helped in good times and in bad . . .
May we have friends to stand by us in joy and sorrow . . .
And may the Lord bless us with happy years so we may enjoy his kingdom life
for ever . . .

CYCLE C

3rd Sunday of Ordinary Time (Lk 1:1-4, 4:14-21)

REFLECTING

Like the gospel writer Luke, we are called to carefully "trace the whole sequence of events," the moments in our lives when people have spoken to us of Jesus, the moments we have experienced the presence of God. Luke wrote about these events; we speak of them by the way we live our lives.

In this gospel, we see Jesus returning to his hometown of Nazareth and entering the synagogue on the Sabbath as he was in the habit of doing. (How well have we formed the habit of going to church on Sunday to pray and celebrate with our faith community?)

Jesus stood to read the scripture. He unrolled the scroll. As we listen to his word at our Sunday liturgy, so the people in his village heard him speak the words of the prophet Isaiah. As he finished speaking, they sat with their eyes fixed on him eagerly awaiting his homily.

How eager are we to hear the word of God? How enthusiastically will we speak this word? And as a family, how joyfully do we welcome travelers, strangers and friends into our Sunday Mass celebration? Luke's Good News offers us moments for reflection.

TALKING

1. Talk about hospitality. Suggest ways you can make people feel more comfortable and welcome in your home and in church.

2. Share your answers:
   For me, Sunday Mass is _____.
   I find it _____ to listen to the word of God because _____.

DOING

1. As a family "trace the whole sequence of events" that have helped form you as Christians. Begin with members of your family tree.

2. Make your weekly scripture symbol—a scroll. Place it in your home or on your SUNDAY THROUGHOUT THE YEAR banner.

PRAYING

(As a family, repeat the words Jesus spoke in the synagogue.)

Leader: The spirit of the Lord has been given to me,
All: (Repeat)
Leader: for he has anointed me.
All: (Repeat)
Leader: He has sent me to bring the good news to the poor,
All: (Repeat)
Leader: to proclaim liberty to captives,
All: (Repeat)
Leader: and to the blind new sight,
All: (Repeat)
Leader: to set the downtrodden free,
All: (Repeat)
Leader: to proclaim the Lord's year of favor.
All: (Repeat)

Jan 23, 1983 / Jan 26, 1986 / Jan 22, 1989

4th Sunday of Ordinary Time (Lk 4:21-30)

REFLECTING

Have you ever forgotten an answer on a test? Have you ever forgotten to do something you were supposed to do? Have you ever forgotten a promise you made to a friend? Have you ever forgotten a promise you made to God?

Sometimes we forget we are called by God to live as his people. We live as lost people. Prophets help us to remember who we are. Prophets are people who are willing to be unpopular, to be laughed at and ridiculed. They are willing to do God's will and not their own. They are even willing to suffer and die.

Jesus was a prophet. How dejected he must have felt the first time he preached in his hometown of Nazareth! At first his townspeople marveled at his preaching. Then they discovered that he intended to teach others, even the Gentiles.

The people were enraged. They wanted to be exclusive. Jesus reminded them of two people from the Old Testament, the widow of Zarephath to whom the prophet Elijah was sent and of the leper Naaman whom the prophet Elisha healed, in order to show that God's call extended beyond the Chosen people. Even with a mile walk outside the city to cool their tempers, the people remained "filled with indignation." In their anger they even wanted to throw Jesus over the side of a hill. They did not understand that God had sent Jesus to teach *every* man and woman.

TALKING

1. Talk about the qualities of a prophet. Who is your favorite prophet from the Old Testament, the New Testament or today? Why? What media and what message might a prophet of today choose to help our world?

2. How do you think Jesus felt about being rejected by the people who were his friends and neighbors as a young boy? What were the different responses that Jesus could have given to the townspeople?

3. Share your answers:
   When I am rejected by my friends, I _____.
   If I were with Jesus when the people became angry, I would have
   _____.

DOING

1. Place a bowl of seeds (pumpkin or any edible seed) in the center of your table. After each dinner meal this week eat some of the seeds as a sign of your willingness to grow in the living of God's call.

2. Make your weekly scripture symbol—the outline of a synagogue. Place it in your home or on your SUNDAY THROUGHOUT THE YEAR banner.

PRAYING

(As a family, sit in silence for a few moment.)

Think of the times you may have rejected one another because of what was said or done. (Pause)
Think of the times you showed your anger. (Pause)
Think of how much you are loved by God and all the members of your family. (Pause)

(Place your hand on the shoulder of each family member in turn. Ask forgiveness for the times you have forgotten to show your love.)

Jan 30, 1983 / Jan 29, 1989

5th Sunday of Ordinary Time (Lk 5:1-11)

REFLECTING

"No more fishing for me," shouted Juan, "I'm going home."

"Me too," answered Philip. "We haven't caught one fish after getting here so early." Juan and Philip slowly gathered their fishing equipment and wearily began their walk home.

Simon Peter, James and John must have been exhausted too after a long night of fishing. While mending and washing their large dragnets, Jesus arrived, got into their boat, and asked these tired men to pull out a short distance from shore so that he could continue to speak to the crowd.

When Jesus had finished speaking, he requested that these fishermen go into deeper water and lower their nets. Impetuous Peter was quick to respond, "Master, we worked hard all night long and caught nothing." Perhaps a little reluctantly, he added, "but if you say so, I will put out the nets." How like Peter we are sometimes, relying solely on ourselves and not allowing God to work through us!

When the nets were filled with fish, the friends were alarmed. As always, Jesus immediately gave comfort, "Do not be afraid." Peter fell to his knees proclaiming his unworthiness.

We too show fear and disbelief when God chooses us as instruments of his work. But Jesus is calling us, too. By our baptism and our confirmation we are committed to him. May God use us to help others follow Jesus.

TALKING

1. What does Jesus mean when he says, "From now on it is men you will catch"? How would you do this?

2. Are you ever afraid to follow Jesus? Do you ever feel unworthy of being his follower? Discuss ways to handle these feelings.

3. Share your answers:
   When I feel unworthy like Peter, I _____.
   When I am afraid, I _____.
   If I had been present for that large catch of fish, I would have
   _____.

DOING

1. Have the family role play this fishing scene. Give reasons for the actions of your character.

2. Make your weekly scripture symbol—a fish. Place it in your home and on your SUNDAY THROUGHOUT THE YEAR banner.

PRAYING

Response: Come after me.
God, you said to Noah, Abraham, Isaac and Jacob ...
You said to Moses, Joseph, kings and prophets ...
Jesus, you said to Peter, John and James ...
You say today to men and women, boys and girls ...

Lord,
You told us to come after you and you would show us a new way to love and a new way to live. As we follow you, show us how to help others to follow you too. Amen.

6th Sunday of Ordinary Time (Lk 6:17, 20-26)

REFLECTING

Jesus taught us the way to happiness: Live the life of the beatitudes. The word "beatitude" means *happiness*; it defines for us a lived faith. We belong to the kingdom of God when we practice the values taught in the beatitudes.

The beatitudes are in sharp contrast to our human and worldly standards of happiness; they offer the challenge to see and welcome God as the center of our life and to live happily now in relationship to God and to all his people. They tell us how to anticipate the total fulfillment of the kingdom in the future.

Like the apostles, we are asked to become a sign of the kingdom for others. We are to free ourselves from anger, from unfriendly words, from impure thoughts. We are to live loneliness with love, fear with hope, turmoil with peace. We are to live joy in the midst of tears.

Charlie Brown sings, "Happiness is coming home again." When we know we belong someplace and to someone, when we realize that alone we can do nothing, when we say yes to God, then we have come home again. Welcome home. The kingdom of God is yours now and forever.

TALKING

1. Reread today's gospel (Lk 6:17-26). Evaluate your living of these beatitudes. What are your strengths? weaknesses?

Be poor in spirit—Are you able to admit to others you need help? Are you open to change? Do you realize you don't have all the answers?

Weep—Do you feel for the hurt of others? Are you able to show your feelings and emotions?

Hunger—Is God present in your daily decisions? Do people come before things? Do you have spiritual goals?

Suffer—Are you able to take criticism or anger at school, home, office without fighting back? Do personal attacks destroy your self-image?

2. Talk about the times you have prayed before doing something. (In Luke, Jesus prays before making any decision.)

3. Share your answers:
   The beatitude I find easiest/hardest to live is _____.
   I was pleased to hear that _____.
   My formula for happiness is _____.

DOING

1. Write a family prayer. Post it in the kitchen as a reminder to talk with God during the week and before every decision.

2. Make your weekly scripture symbol—a smiling face. Place it in your home or on your SUNDAY THROUGHOUT THE YEAR banner.

PRAYING

Thank you, Jesus, for teaching us how to live. We are willing to be poor, to weep, to hunger, to suffer, so that all people can become family members in your Father's home. Be present with us as we try to bring justice, peace and love to others. Amen.

1st Sunday of Lent (Lk 4:1-13)

REFLECTING

At his baptism Jesus was anointed with the Spirit. The Spirit was with Jesus for his desert journey as he resisted the three temptations of the devil and chose to walk the road to Jerusalem not as a great king but as the suffering Son of God.

During Lent we should allow ourselves to be led by the Spirit into our own desert for 40 days. By setting aside quiet moments we can speak with God; we can learn to listen by becoming docile to the Spirit in our life; we can show appreciation for others and by not giving in to our every whim and desire, we can begin to make God and his people the center of our lives.

In our 40 days of desert wanderings let us re-evaluate our lives by asking ourselves where we have been, where we are now and where we are going. As a family, let us provide the home environment necessary for moments of silence and reflection. Together let us live in a spirit of enthusiasm as we prepare for new life.

TALKING

1. Talk about your baptismal promises, your mission, and ways you can allow yourself to be led by the Spirit.

2. Discuss the different things you could resolve to do during Lent. Include positive things to do as well as things to give up.

3. Share your answers with family members:
   As a family, we will pray _____.
   To be in the desert with Jesus, I _____.

DOING

1. Use a cactus plant as a centerpiece to remember and live Christ's desert experience.

2. Make your weekly scripture symbol—the number "40." Place it in your home or on your SUNDAY THROUGHOUT THE YEAR banner.

PRAYING

Response: Lord, walk with us through the desert.
Sometimes we feel lost and alone ...
Sometimes we are afraid and do not know where to go ...
Sometimes we turn away from God and lose our direction ...

Lord,
Send your Spirit to walk with us through these 40 days of Lent. Help us as a family to walk together through difficulties and hardships. Be with us in our desert wanderings as we seek your life. Amen.

2nd Sunday of Lent (Lk 9:28-36)

REFLECTING

In the wonder-experience we look at things we know and really see them for the first time. We are not in control. There is no time. No words are spoken. Just a moment of awe, of wonderment, of the recognition of mystery, of the experience of presence.

In today's gospel we experience with Peter, James and John, the presence of mystery in this transfiguration scene. Like them we are filled with awe as we recognize Jesus in his glory.

The mountain has always been a meeting place between God and us. Here, alone, there are no distractions. Here, our hearts turn to God as we smell the fresh air, hear the quiet, and see the majesty of creation before us. It was on the mountain that God revealed himself to Moses, that Elijah experienced the presence of God in a gentle breeze. It was here on the mountain that the apostles saw Jesus' glory.

May we always be filled with awe in God's presence, filled with faith in the presence of one another.

TALKING

1. With your family, share some of your wonder experiences. Note the similarities in this type of experience.

2. In the wonder experience of his transfiguration, what is Jesus asking us to see, hear and understand? How is he asking us to respond?

3. Share your answers:
   For me, wonder is _____.
   If I had been with the apostles, I would have _____.
   I find hints of the fullness of life to come in _____.

DOING

1. Place a flower pot filled with sand on the table for a centerpiece. Have a slender candle for each family member to light during Praying below. Let the brightness of these candles be a reminder of the dazzling whiteness of Jesus' transfiguration.

2. Make your weekly scripture symbol—a brilliant sun with rays. Place it in your home or on your SUNDAY THROUGHOUT THE YEAR banner.

PRAYING

(Begin with each family member holding an unlighted candle.)

Lord,
You tell us you are the Son of God, and like your three friends, we are astonished. Lord, help us to have wonder in our lives, to be astonished by mystery, to surrender to the unknown. Help us to look at everything as if we were seeing it for the first time.

You are wonder-filled! May we begin to experience the wonder of you in our daily life.

We light our candles as a sign of the dazzling whiteness of your presence in our life.

(As you light each family member's candle say, "(*Name*), be wonder-filled." After all the candles are lighted, place them in the centerpiece.)

CYCLE C

3rd Sunday of Lent (Lk 13:1-9)

REFLECTING

"Our administration will offer new reforms in politics, education, health and business," reads the morning newspaper. "Vote for us."

How often we have heard these words promising reform! In today's gospel, Jesus calls each of us to change. He tells us that unless we reform we will come to the same end as those killed accidentally by the falling tower or those treated cruelly by Pilate in a revolt at the Temple. Jesus does not condemn these unfortunate victims but uses their tragedy as a warning of what we bring upon ourselves when we live turned away from God.

How dejected Jesus must have felt sometimes. After he had been preaching for three years, the people still refused to respond to his message. Yet he continued to believe in their ability to change. How easy it is to understand the parable of the fig tree. For three years this tree had grown in the vineyard but had produced no fruit. "Cut it down," ordered the owner (God). The foreman (Jesus) pleaded for another year "to dig around it and manure it."

The message of Jesus during this Lenten season and all seasons calls for our *immediate* response. There is an urgency, for there is little time left. We must begin to bear fruit in the work of the Lord. We must begin *now* to reform and repent.

TALKING

1. Discuss ways to bear fruit during the remaining three weeks of Lent. Begin *now*.
2. Share your answers with family members:
   After reading this gospel, I feel _____.
   I will begin to reform now by _____.

DOING

1. Call a friend you have not seen in a long time. Write a letter to your grandmother, grandfather or a relative who lives away.

2. Make your weekly scripture symbol—a bare tree. Place it in your home or on your SUNDAY THROUGHOUT THE YEAR banner.

PRAYING

Lord,
The time passes so quickly. Another day comes and goes and we forget to be with you and with your people. You remind us, Lord, to begin to act *now*, to begin to reform. Help us not wait for tomorrow. Help our family to live with you daily in our lives. Amen.

4th Sunday of Lent (Lk 15:1-3, 11-32)

REFLECTING

"I love you no matter what, no matter how you look or what you do or say. I love you no matter what your weaknesses or limitations. I love you not only when you please me or when you achieve something. I love you simply because you are a worthwhile and lovable person."

We are freed to try and love in this way only because we have first experienced the unconditional love of God our Father. We see this type of love which God has for us in today's gospel story of a father's love for his two sons. The younger son leaves home, squanders his possessions and rejects his family. The father welcomes and forgives this younger son at the first sign of his return and shows his joy through a celebration. How beautiful for a father to show love through forgiveness!

The older son, who has faithfully remained with the father at home, becomes angry. He feels slighted. Like the older son we sometimes forget that God offers his unconditional love to all, regardless of the way we have behaved. In this story we discover that God's love extends to *all* people, not only the Chosen People represented by the older son. All people are his people.

God is our loving and protecting, rejoicing and forgiving Father. How good it is to know that God our Father awaits us with open arms whenever we decide to turn back to him. How beautiful it is to experience a no-matter-what love, the unconditional love of God our Father.

TALKING

1. When we do wrong we turn away from God. When our relationship with God is not right, our relationship with others and with ourselves is broken. Examine together your relationship with God, with others and with yourself. Talk about ways to reconcile broken relationships.

2. Talk about God as a loving Father. Discuss ways you can begin to offer the unconditional love of God to others.

3. Share your answers:
   I break my relationship with God, with others or with myself when I _____.
   To turn back to God and his people, I would _____.
   God shows his love by _____; my family shows love by _____.

DOING

1. Role play this forgiveness story. Afterward, have the characters give the reasons for their actions.

2. Make your weekly scripture symbol—a smiling face with outstretched arms. Place it in your home or on your SUNDAY THROUGHOUT THE YEAR banner.

PRAYING

"I will leave this place and go to my father and say: Father, I have sinned against heaven and against you."

(Think about these words of scripture. Silently reflect on what you have done or what you have failed to do. After reflecting, ask forgiveness for any hurt you may have caused another member of the family. Then offer a sign of forgiveness to each family member.)

Mar 13, 1983 / Mar 9, 1986 / Mar 5, 1989

CYCLE C

5th Sunday of Lent (Jn 8:1-11)

REFLECTING

How humiliating it is to be singled out when you have done something wrong. Everyone stares at you. You feel like crying. Somehow you find the courage to stand there.

The woman in today's gospel must have felt the same humiliation as she was brought forward and made to stand in front of everyone. Everyone stared. Many pointed an accusing finger at her while others whispered to one another the wrongs she had done.

The crowd shouted that she should be stoned for committing adultery. Without speaking a word, Jesus leaned over and began tracing on the ground with his finger. Could he have been writing the sins of this woman? The crowd persisted in their shouts, "Stone her."

"If there is one of you who has not sinned, let him be the first to throw a stone at her," replied Jesus as he began to write again. Perhaps he wrote the sins of the crowd. By slowly walking away, the people in the crowd confessed their guilt.

Jesus never condemns a person; he only condemns the sin. He offered the woman mercy and understanding. He forgave her and called for her conversion, just as he also calls for our conversion. Let us not disappoint him.

TALKING

1. Discuss what you think Jesus wrote in the sand.

2. Talk about the ways in which you pass judgment on others. How do you help yourself and others turn to Christ?

3. Share your answers:
   When someone passes judgment on me, I _____.
   The thing I find hardest to forgive in someone is _____.
   I am like this crowd when I _____.

DOING

1. Examine your conscience. What did I do? Why did I do it? What am I going to do about it? Plan to celebrate the sacrament of reconciliation this week.

2. Make your weekly scripture symbol—a stone. Place it in your home or on your SUNDAY THROUGHOUT THE YEAR banner.

PRAYING

Response: Lord, forgive us.
For the times we have talked about others in unkind ways . . .
For the times we have laughed at others . . .
For the times we passed judgment on others . . .
For the times we have thought so much of ourselves that we forgot to think of you . . .
(Add your own petitions.)

Thank you for your forgiveness, Lord. In your mercy we are made new again. We continue to follow in your footsteps toward the new life of the resurrection. Amen.

Passion Sunday (Lk 19:29-40, the Procession)

REFLECTING

Jerusalem was having a festival. People came from miles around. Like all good practicing Jews, Jesus went up to Jerusalem to celebrate the Passover.

The authorities were upset with Jesus' preaching and with his latest incident, the raising of Lazarus from the dead. The crowd's enthusiasm for Jesus, however, had increased. As Jesus triumphantly entered Jerusalem riding on a donkey, surrounded by waving palms, the people proclaimed their joy:

> *"Blessings on the King who comes,*
> *in the name of the Lord!*
> Peace in heaven
> and glory in the highest heavens!"*

Jesus asked to ride a donkey as a sign of his humility; he asked for an unridden one as a sign that his mission was one only he could perform. Just as the people missed the messianic humility of Jesus riding an ass, so also they failed to understand that he must suffer. Jesus entered the city of Jerusalem knowing his life was in danger.

The same people who joyfully shouted "Hosanna" for his entry quickly disappeared when the authorities arrested Jesus. Would our faith have stood the test?

(This Reflecting is based on the gospel commemorating our Lord's entrance into Jerusalem. As a family, plan to read or tell the story of the passion: Lk 22:14-23:56.)

TALKING

1. Talk about Jesus going up to Jerusalem. Through your senses, try to experience his triumphant entry. Place yourself in the scene. Share your insights with family members.

2. How are you able to grow in your faith? Would your faith have stood the test? Recall the events of the passion. At what point would you have found it difficult to stand by Jesus?

3. Share your answers:
   I am like the people of Jerusalem when I _____.
   I am like the authorities of Jerusalem when I _____.

DOING

1. Choose different things to do as a family during Holy Week, for example *Monday*, *Tuesday*, *Wednesday*—In keeping with an ancient tradition, vigorously clean your home on these days.
Holy Thursday—Have a passover meal.
Good Friday—Have an hour of silence.
Holy Saturday—Review your Lenten resolutions. Bake Easter breads. Dye Easter eggs.
Easter—Decorate home with fresh flowers. Have an Easter egg hunt. Sing and rejoice.

2. Make your weekly scripture symbol—a palm. Place it in your home or on your SUNDAY THROUGHOUT THE YEAR banner.

PRAYING

Lord,
You entered Jerusalem in such glory! It is sad to think that the same people that welcomed you soon turned away from you.

How often do we turn away from you too? We forget to pray, to celebrate you, to thank you, to live with you in our daily lives.

Give us the courage to walk by you on your way to Calvary.

Mar 27, 1983 / Mar 23, 1986 / Mar 19, 1989

CYCLE C

2nd Sunday of Easter (Jn 20:19-31)

REFLECTING

Jesus, risen and glorified, brings us his peace. When the frightened disciples locked themselves in a room to hide from the Jews, Jesus came among them and said, "Peace be with you," and they were filled with joy. Peace and joy are qualities we associate with the risen Lord.

Today we receive the peace and joy of Christ through the Spirit in the sacrament of reconciliation. In today's gospel we hear the words of Christ as he instituted this sacrament of his forgiveness:

"Receive the Holy Spirit.
For those whose sins you forgive,
they are forgiven;
for those whose sins you retain,
they are retained."

Let us always remember that only when we turn to Jesus can we experience true joy and true peace. He forgives us through the sacrament of reconciliation today and brings us healing, joy and peace.

TALKING

1. Imagine that you are one of the disciples in the upper room. You don't understand what has happened to Jesus; you are afraid the Jews will kill you too. Then Jesus appears and says, "Peace be with you." What is your response? How do you feel?

2. What role does the sacrament of reconciliation play in the life of your family?

3. Share your answers:
   I am most aware of the peace and joy of the risen Lord when

   _____.

   The word "reconciliation" bring to mind _____.
   I share in Jesus' forgiveness when _____.

DOING

1. Write a family prayer of forgiveness. Use it in Praying (below).

2. Make your weekly scripture symbol—an olive branch for peace. Place it in your home or on your SUNDAY THROUGHOUT THE YEAR banner.

PRAYING

(As a family, say the prayer of forgiveness you wrote in Doing #1. Then offer the kiss of peace to each member of the family and say, "Peace be with you.")

3rd Sunday of Easter (Jn 21:1-19)

REFLECTING

We realize in today's gospel how close and intimate our friendship with Christ can be: "Do you love me?" "Yes, Lord, you know that I love you." We receive encouragement in our mission to preach the Good News from Jesus, our friend and brother.

In his third post-resurrection appearance Jesus came to his friends at the side of the lake. He prepared breakfast and ate with them. Meals are for friends. We can learn about others during a meal.

During this early morning meal, Peter pledged his love and received the task of protecting and leading the followers of Jesus. He also discovered that he would suffer and die a martyr's death for his beliefs.

As a friend of Jesus, we too are asked to follow him. Like Peter we may be asked to suffer for what we believe. And again like Peter, we are asked to tell Jesus that we love him.

TALKING

1. How do you show that you love someone?

2. If you had been present that morning, would you have been filled with awe and wonder? fear and disbelief? welcome and acceptance? Why?

3. Share your answers:
   In what ways do people ask, "Do you love me?" _____.
   If I had been present at this lakeside breakfast I would have

   _____.

DOING

1. Have family members volunteer to prepare a special breakfast.

2. Make your weekly scripture symbol—a fish over a fire. Place it in your home or on your SUNDAY THROUGHOUT THE YEAR banner.

PRAYING

Response: Lord, you know that I love you.

For coming into our lives and for offering yourself as a friend to each of us . . .
For the food that we eat, for the meals that we share, and the understanding we
   receive, for your gift to us in the Eucharist . . .
For the courage to believe and the strength to suffer sometimes for that belief . . .

(Offer each family member a sign of your love.)

CYCLE C

4th Sunday of Easter (Jn 10:27-30)

REFLECTING

> The night is dark, and I am far from home,
> Lead thou me on,
> Keep thou my feet; I do not ask to see
> The distant scene; one step enough for me.
>
> —J. H. Newman

We ask Jesus our shepherd to daily lead us, one step at a time toward the fullness of life with him. Protected and nourished by him, we allow ourselves to be guided. Trusting in his direction, we become docile, relying totally upon him.

As his sheep, we belong to Jesus. We have been given to him by the Father. It is impossible for Jesus to lose us; impossible for others to take us away from him. Jesus laid down his life for us; he is the Good Shepherd. We, his sheep, belong to him forever.

We also belong to one another. Together we grow in his life and share in his gift to us, eternal life. Let us walk together, for we are far from home and the night is sometimes very dark and frightening. It is so easy to lose our way, to lose sight of the distant scene. Good Shepherd, lead us on together.

TALKING

1. Our culture is not a pastoral one. What occupations today hold the same meaning as shepherd held in Jesus' time?

2. Share your answers:
   I try to follow the Good Shepherd by _____.
   When I think of Jesus as my shepherd and friend, I _____.

DOING

1. Make a shepherd's staff from a fallen tree limb. Hang it in the kitchen with a paper scroll attached that says, "I am the Good Shepherd."

2. Make your weekly scripture symbol—a sheep. Place it in your home or on your SUNDAY THROUGHOUT THE YEAR banner.

PRAYING

Jesus, our shepherd and our friend, We thank (*names of people who help guide you*) for they help guide us toward you. May we remember that we are all your people. Remain our Good Shepherd forever. Amen.

Apr 24, 1983 / Apr 20, 1986 / Apr 16, 1989

5th Sunday of Easter (Jn 13:31-33a, 34-35)

REFLECTING

All of us are called to love and be loved. How beautiful is the moment when we discover that we are not only capable of loving another but that we can be loved by another!

In today's gospel Jesus gives us a new commandment: Love as I have loved. All of God's rules for life can be expressed in this one single command. If we wonder how to evaluate our love for another, we find the answer in this command of Jesus. "Love your neighbor as yourself" seems easy when placed next to this new command, Love as I have loved.

Jesus' love for his disciples should be our guide. We should be recognized as followers of Jesus, as were the first disciples, by the love we have for one another.

Let us begin to put on the love of Jesus.

TALKING

1. Have each family member mention one event in the life of Jesus which showed his love for someone.
2. How could you put on the love of Jesus?
3. Share your answers:
   To love as Jesus loved, I _____.
   I find it hard to love when _____.

DOING

1. Read *The Giving Tree,* by Shel Silverstein. (New York: Harper and Row, 1964).
2. For your weekly scripture symbol—outline a figure of Jesus and place a heart on the figure. Place it in your home or on your SUNDAY THROUGHOUT THE YEAR banner.

PRAYING

Silently list all the people who love you. (Pause)
Silently list all the people you love. (Pause)

Thank you, God, for loving us and showing us how to love. Thank you for giving us the ability to love you, others and ourselves. When we love, we begin to know you better for you are love. Let us go now as a family and love. Amen.

6th Sunday of Easter (Jn 14:23-29)

REFLECTING

Be a maker of peace and make gentle
the ways of this world.
Walk in peace.
Work in peace.
Live in peace.
Be with another in peace.
Be with yourself in peace.
Peace is active.
Doing something.
Making something.
Becoming one with God and one with
all the people he has made.
"My friend, I give you my peace."

—Peace,
a Reflection film, Ikonographics

In the tender and emotional farewell at the Last Supper, Jesus tells his friends not to be fearful at his departure:
"the Holy Spirit,
whom the Father will send in my name,
will teach you everything
and remind you of all I have said to you."

Jesus gives the gift of peace, his peace, to all his friends. This is an inner peace which our world may not understand, a deep inside oneness.

TALKING

1. How is peace active? List ways you can be a maker of peace.
2. When Jesus helped or forgave someone, he said, "Go in peace." Why?
3. "Blessed are the peacemakers, they shall be called children of God." Discuss this beatitude.
4. Share your answers:
   For my family living, peace means _____.
   I walk in peace when I _____.

DOING

1. Make a collage of magazine pictures of people at peace. Across the top write, "We are peacemakers."
2. Make your weekly scripture symbol—the word "Peace." Place it in your home or on your SUNDAY THROUGHOUT THE YEAR banner.

PRAYING

Lord,
We are your family. We try to live in peace with one another; we trust one another. Sometimes we are afraid. Sometimes our world laughs at the way we try to live, and we forget that your Spirit is with us. In our family living, help us always to be sensitive to the needs of one another, to offer and receive forgiveness. Make us your peacemakers.

(Place your hand on the shoulder of each family member and say:
(*Name*), remember, the peace of Jesus is yours.)

May 8, 1983 / May 4, 1986 / Apr 30, 1989

7th Sunday of Easter (Jn 17:20-26)

REFLECTING

The warm, loving John XXIII opened his heart and life to embrace the world. He tenderly called us his children and invited the world to become one. We can almost hear him pleading with us to love one another and to see what unites us, not what separates us.

This is the same plea which Jesus makes to us in today's gospel. In this tender prayer to his Father for the unity of his church, we are asked to become signs of the love that exists between the Father and the Son. Our love for one another is the sign that the world may believe.

We need not be overwhelmed by this challenge for we have a love model before us. God lives in Jesus; they are one. Jesus sees himself as a gift, a gift of the Father's love, a love that was present before the world began. Since Jesus lives in his friends, in each of us, God lives in us, too. In this life, we imitate the unconditional love of Father and Son; we model their love. We, too, are a gift.

The Mass is our prayer of unity. Here we assert that unity is possible. In this gathered assembly, we remember our mission as we call God our Father and receive Jesus, the gift of the Father. Here we offer a sign of peace, of oneness, to God's people, and we see what unites, not what separates us from one another.

TALKING

1. Talk about ways to achieve unity. How can we become signs of love so that the world will believe?
2. Share your answers:
   As a gift of love, I will _____.
   Jesus' prayer to his Father makes me feel _____ because _____.

DOING

1. Make and display a brightly-colored construction paper chain of unity. Use it during Praying.
2. Make your weekly scripture symbol—a unity sign. Place it in your home or on your SUNDAY THROUGHOUT THE YEAR banner.

PRAYING

(Hold the chain of unity you made in Doing #1.)

Your love makes us one, God. By our presence, help us to be love signs to a separated world. We pray that all may be one as you are one with your Son. May your love for your Son live in us. As a sign of our oneness, we hold our chain of unity and pray the prayer your Son taught us: Our Father, . . .

CYCLE C

Trinity Sunday (Jn 16:12-15)

REFLECTING

Father, ...
We joyfully proclaim our faith
in the mystery of your Godhead.
You have revealed your glory
as the glory also of your Son
and of the Holy Spirit:
three Persons equal in majesty,
undivided in splendor,
yet one Lord, one God,
ever to be adored in your everlasting glory.

—from the Preface of the
Mass of the Holy Trinity

The Trinity is a sign of unity, a sign of the mutual love, life and communion of the Father, Son and Holy Spirit. To live the life of the Trinity is to live in peace, harmony and love with one another. In today's gospel, Jesus announced that the Spirit of truth would come to help us understand the life of the Father, Son and Holy Spirit.

At the opening of the Mass, the priest welcomes us: "The grace of our Lord *Jesus Christ* and the love of *God* and the fellowship of the *Holy Spirit* be with you all." Together in unity we respond: "And also with you." We celebrate the life of the Trinity together.

In the Trinity the activity of the Father is creation; the Son, redemption; the Holy Spirit, revelation. Whenever we partake in the activities of creating, healing and revealing, we are living the life of the Trinity. It is the prayer of Jesus that all may be one as he and the Father and the Spirit are one.

TALKING

1. Discuss the words in the prayer of Jesus that all may be one as he and the Father and the Spirit are one.

2. As a family, recall prayers and songs which speak of the life of the Trinity.

DOING

1. Write a family prayer of belief in the Trinity. Profess your faith by proclaiming this prayer as you begin each day.

2. Make your weekly scripture symbol—a trefoil. Place it in your home or on your SUNDAY THROUGHOUT THE YEAR banner.

PRAYING

God,
You sent your Son and together with him in mutual love, the Holy Spirit. May we praise and honor you always by saying:

Glory be to the Father
and
to the Son
and
to the Holy Spirit.

As it was in the beginning, is now,
and ever shall be, world without end. Amen.

(Extend your hands over the members of the family and bless them.)

May 29, 1983 / May 25, 1986 / May 21, 1989

Solemnity of Corpus Christi (Lk 9:11b-17)

REFLECTING

In this great sacrament you feed your people
and strengthen them in holiness, ...
We come then to this wonderful sacrament
to be fed at your table
and grow into the likeness of the risen Christ.

—from the Preface for Corpus Christi

At one time the people in the divided church of Corinth were not growing into the likeness of Christ. In today's second reading (1 Cor 11:23-26) Paul admonishes them for their lack of charity and good manners in celebrating the Eucharist. They would gather together in the setting of a fraternal meal to break bread together. To this meal different groups brought food, but chose carefully the people with whom they would share their food. Some people overindulged while others went home hungry. Paul recalled for them the Last Supper and the oneness they are called to have in the body and blood of Christ.

Jesus comes to us in the meal of the Eucharist. In this bread and wine, in this body and blood of Jesus, we have the sign of God's presence with us. Without this meal, we are divided, homeless, without life. With this bread, we are made one and have the life that will go on forever. With this meal we are strengthened until Jesus comes again.

Let us reflect on the way we celebrate the meal of the Eucharist with one another.

TALKING

1. Talk about the good manners, respect and charity that should be present in all celebrations of the Eucharist. If Paul were present in your church today, what would he say?

2. As a family, reflect on your participation, celebration and reception of the Eucharist.

3. Share your answers:
    To grow in the likeness of Christ, I will _____.
    For me, the meal of the Eucharist is _____.
    In faith, I proclaim _____.

DOING

1. Prepare a special family meal. Choose music, readings and prayers to conclude the meal. Bake bread and share it as a sign of your oneness.

2. Make your weekly scripture symbol—a loaf of bread. Place it in your home or on your SUNDAY THROUGHOUT THE YEAR banner.

PRAYING

(Process around your home singing this acclamation:)
When we eat this bread
and drink this cup
We proclaim your death, Lord Jesus,
until you come in glory.

CYCLE C

9th Sunday of Ordinary Time (Lk 7:1-10)

REFLECTING

Sometimes when someone who is very dear to us becomes ill we do not know what to do or where to turn. We reach out desperately to help. We send for a doctor and pray that healing will take place.

In today's gospel, the Roman soldier, a centurion, discovered that his favorite servant was near death and he immediately turned to Jesus for help. As always, Jesus responded immediately to someone in need and traveled to the centurion's home.

As Jesus neared the home, friends were sent by the centurion with this request: "Sir, do not put yourself to trouble; because I am not worthy to have you under my roof; and for this same reason I do not presume to come to you myself; but give the word and let my servant be cured." One can imagine the surprise and wonderment of Jesus. This man's faith was beyond any Jesus had found in Israel. Through his word, Jesus healed the servant, just as he continues to heal all people of faith today.

The centurion saw God's presence among his people in Jesus. Every time we celebrate Mass, we are called to recognize Jesus in the Eucharist in this same way. Through his word we too are healed.

TALKING

1. With family members, talk about your faith. Recall the act of faith made for you at your baptism. Share the words of a personal act of faith you now make in your life.

2. What word or words of Jesus bring healing to you when you are troubled?

3. Share your answers:
   I see God's presence in _____.
   My faith helps me to _____.
   I am most like the centurion when I _____.

DOING

1. Write words of comfort and prayers of healing to those in your family or community who are sick.

2. Make your weekly scripture symbol—a house with the word "Faith" inside. Place it in your home or on your SUNDAY THROUGHOUT THE YEAR banner.

PRAYING

(Reflect on the words we speak before Communion. In humility and hope, proclaim them as a family.)

This is the Lamb of God who takes away the sins of the world. Happy are those who are called to his supper.

Lord, I am not worthy to receive you. But only say the word and I shall be healed.

10th Sunday of Ordinary Time (Lk 7:11-17)

REFLECTING

> Through this holy anointing
> may the Lord in his love and mercy help you
>   with the grace of the Holy Spirit. Amen.
> May the Lord who frees you from sin
> save you and raise you up. Amen.
>
> —No. 76, Rite of Anointing

With these words, the priest anoints the sick with oil. In this sacrament of anointing of the sick we show our concern as a community for the sick and dying. We are encouraged to ask for anointing for those who are dangerously ill due to sickness or old age, those having surgery due to a dangerous illness, the elderly if they are in a weak condition even if no dangerous illness is present, the sick children if they have sufficient understanding to be comforted by the sacrament.

The anointing of the sick is a community action. It is the gesture of the entire community in showing its concern, in offering its support and prayers, in expressing its common faith to the sick who may be doubting and alone.

Jesus spent his life caring for the sick—the physically, mentally and spiritually ill. He brought warmth and compassion to them. He offered comfort. In today's gospel we experience this deep compassion of Jesus in his response to the grieving widow of Nain over the death of her only son: "Do not cry." Then, in silence, he reached out his hands to heal.

We are responsible toward people who are sick. We are called as a community to take a stand against people dying alone, against suffering alone. As the crowd of townspeople was present to the grieving widow, so let us be present to the sick and dying and continue the work of Christ as a concerned and comforting community.

TALKING

1. Reflect and share your personal attitude toward the sick and dying. Discuss ways the family could help these people in the community.

2. Picture the healing scene in Nain. Place yourself in the story. Are you a member of the crowd that accompanied Jesus, a member of the crowd with the widow, or simply a passerby? How do you feel? Describe what you see. Share your response to this healing.

3. Share your answers:
   When the healed son began to talk, I think he said these words:
   _____.
   I show my compassion by _____.

DOING

1. Write a family prayer and choose ritual actions to show concern for the sick in your family. Become familiar with the rite of the anointing. As a family, plan to attend a communal anointing of the sick.

2. Make your weekly scripture symbol—a hand. Place it in your home or on your SUNDAY THROUGHOUT THE YEAR banner.

PRAYING

Lord,
You showed compassion for the people and walked among them doing good and healing the sick. In your kindness, hear our prayers.

Give strength to our friends who are not well, especially (*names*).

Jun 8, 1986 / Jun 11, 1989

11th Sunday of Ordinary Time (Lk 7:36-8:3)

REFLECTING

Do we recognize the need for forgiveness in our lives? Have we ever experienced heal-ing by saying we are sorry? Do we know the joy and peace that come by admitting the wrong we have done?

David readily admitted his wrong when confronted by the prophet Nathan in the first reading (2 Sm 12:7-10, 13) and then in the responsorial psalm praised all people who recognize their guilt. It is only in acknowledging our wrongs that guilt can be removed and we can experience joy and gladness.

Because the woman in today's gospel has been forgiven much, her love is great. She expresses her love through signs of welcome and hospitality. She offers a kiss of greet-ing. She anoints Jesus' feet with perfume. (It was an expression of esteem for a guest to have his head anointed with oil.) With her tears, she washes the feet of Jesus and dries them with her hair. (It was the custom for the host to offer water for cleaning dusty feet.) The host Simon seems as unaware of performing these courtesies as he does of recognizing his need for repentance and forgiveness.

Let us pray that we recognize our need for repentance and forgiveness.

TALKING

1. Talk about the customs today which show greeting and hospitality.

2. How do you handle guilt? Share an experience of joy resulting from offering or ask-ing for forgiveness.

3. Share your answer:
   I am most like this woman when I _____.
   Because I have been forgiven, I show my love by _____.
   I find myself being like Simon when I _____.

DOING

1. Have one family member read today's gospel while other family members pantomime the parts. Then have each person explain what his or her character was thinking and feeling during the scene.

2. Make your weekly scripture symbol—a per-fume bottle. Place it in your home or on your SUNDAY THROUGHOUT THE YEAR banner.

PRAYING

Response: Lord, forgive the wrong I have done.

Lord,
Help us recognize our need for forgiveness by saying . . .
Help us heal the guilt we feel by saying . . .
Help us experience joy and peace by saying . . .

Lord,
We know how much you love us. Thank you for showing us how to live like David and the woman who anointed your feet. Be our dinner guest always.

(Anoint family members with perfumed oil.)

Jun 12, 1983 / Jun 15, 1986 / Jun 18, 1989

12th Sunday of Ordinary Time (Lk 9:18-24)

REFLECTING

> (*Name*), you have become a new creation,
> and have clothed yourself in Christ.
>
> —Rite of Baptism

Through our baptism we have become clothed with Christ. We are one in Jesus. When we gather to celebrate the Eucharist as a community of believers, each of us stands tall. Color, race, sex, status—those things which we may think make us different—no longer exist. Our baptism makes us one. Our common faith in Jesus makes each of us a new creation.

Together we share Christ's call to take up our cross *daily* and follow him. Luke is the only gospel writer who stresses that we must do this daily. Each of us knows the experience of being rejected by a friend or laughed at because of something we said or did. We have days when everything seems to go wrong, when it just seems too hard to do our school or business work. Some days when we choose thoughts and actions which are not Christlike, we even become disappointed in ourselves. It is not easy to take up our crosses daily and try to live a life for God and his people. Yet this is the mission that we all share.

TALKING

1. Share your recollection of the baptism of each of the children in the family. Through baptism you share in the priesthood of Jesus. In what ways could you minister as a priest to others?

2. Consider what it means for you to take up your cross daily. Talk about ways to handle your crosses in a life-sustaining way.

3. Share your answers:
   To deny self, I would _____.
   I show I am a member of the community of Jesus by _____.

DOING

1. Make a family baptismal stole. Place the names of family members, a sign of your faith, your family surname, and the words "We are one" on a strip of white material.

2. Make your weekly scripture symbol—a white garment with a cross on it. Place it in your home or on your SUNDAY THROUGHOUT THE YEAR banner.

PRAYING

(Form a circle. Place your hand—or the stole from Doing #1—on the shoulder of each family member and say: "(*Name*), you have become a new creation and clothed yourself in Christ." Then say the following prayer together.)

Lord,
In the white garment we received at our baptism we see the outward sign of our Christian dignity. Thank you for inviting us to be clothed in your likeness. Let us help one another to walk daily in your life and to carry our crosses as we celebrate your presence among us. Let us always experience our oneness in faith through baptism. Amen.

CYCLE C

Jun 19, 1983 / Jun 22, 1986 / Jun 25, 1989

13th Sunday of Ordinary Time (Lk 9:51-62)

REFLECTING

God calls us to be his people. He calls each of us by name.

In today's first reading (1 Kgs 19:16-21) and gospel we hear of the immediate response to his call that is demanded. There are to be no excuses. We can delay no longer. As with the prophet Elisha or some of the would-be followers of Jesus, we can no longer postpone our commitment.

Luke saw Jesus as a prophet, commissioned and consecrated for his work. Jesus wears the cloak of God. Though prophets were not anointed as kings were in the Old Testament, it is interesting to see that Elijah placed his cloak on the shoulders of the young farmer Elisha as a sign of prophet succession and consecration.

We, too, are called to wear the prophet's mantle and to walk in the footsteps of Jesus—to travel to Jerusalem, to the cross and then to resurrection. We are to be dedicated and single-minded in our purpose. We are to put our hand to the plow and not look back or become distracted from our mission.

Let us firmly resolve to encourage one another through love and mutual support so that we can travel the road of faith together.

TALKING

1. Talk about the role of prophet. How was Jesus a prophet? How are you a prophet? How can you keep your hand to the plow?

2. In what ways do you pass on your prophet heritage? Your family heritage?

3. Share your answers:
   My excuse for not following Jesus right now is _____.
   When someone tears me down with biting words, I _____.

DOING

1. Make a map of Jesus' journey to Jerusalem. On the map, place signs of the sayings and stories told on his travels. (Luke begins the *travel narrative* of his gospel with today's Good News.)

2. Make your weekly scripture symbol—a plow. Place it in your home or on your SUNDAY THROUGHOUT THE YEAR banner.

PRAYING

Leader: Lord, we promise to walk in your footsteps.
All: (Repeat)

Leader: We will put our hand to the plow.
All: (Repeat)

Leader: We will be your prophets.
All: (Repeat)

Leader: We will speak your words and live your love.
All: (Repeat)

Leader: We will be signs of your presence to others.
All: (Repeat)

Leader: We will wear the cloak of God.
All: (Repeat)

14th Sunday of Ordinary Time (Lk 10:1-9)

REFLECTING

We walk together on a journey of faith.
We take neither staff
   nor sandals
   nor coat
   nor money for this journey.
We take nothing but faith.

We are like the disciples that Jesus sent before him to offer peace to every town he was to visit. We walk in faith. It would be easy to lose our way but we have the disciples, men and women who have walked before us in loneliness and fear, doubt and rejection; men and women who have walked with courage and hope, with determination and joy. Their footprints are everywhere. We need only open our eyes to see the path and open our hearts to walk its way.

Jesus sent the disciples in pairs to offer peace to others. How joyful we should be to share and work together in our peace mission.

Our mission may not be to foreign lands or even places away from our neighborhood. Our peace mission could simply be seeing and accepting all people as our brothers and sisters regardless of race or color.

We are sent to pre-evangelize, to prepare the people to hear the word of God and accept it in their lives. We provide an environment of welcome and an atmosphere of trust. In our offering of peace, we free others to be created anew. And, like the disciples, we take pride in doing God's will and are joyful that our names are inscribed in heaven.

TALKING

1. You have only a knapsack for a journey. What would you choose to take in your knapsack? Share the reasons for your choices.

2. Recall a time you worked with someone else. Could you have done the job alone? What did this person bring to your shared work?

3. Share your answers:
   My faith journey has taken me through _____.
   I offer peace to another by _____.
   I feel my mission is to _____.

DOING

1. Write a family greeting of peace. Offer this greeting to one another and to friends.

2. Make your weekly scripture symbol—an outline of two people walking on a road. Place it in your home or on your SUNDAY THROUGHOUT THE YEAR banner.

PRAYING

(Raise your hearts and heads toward God for this Irish blessing.)
May the road rise up to meet you.
May the wind be always at your back.
May the sun shine warm upon your face.
And the rains fall soft upon your field and home.
And as we walk together, may God hold you in the palm of his hand. Amen.

Jul 3, 1983 / Jul 6, 1986 / Jul 9, 1989

CYCLE C

15th Sunday of Ordinary Time (Lk 10:25-37)

REFLECTING

Private jets landed carrying celebrities from the West Coast. Busses arrived with a group from the East Coast ready to mobilize the youth to patrol the streets. People across the United States wore green ribbons, a sign of their prayer and plea to end the terror as the number of young children murdered in a Southern city passed 20. At a benefit performance a noted performer was quoted as saying, "Have a heart, honorable people still outnumber dishonorable deeds."

These honorable people are our good neighbors. They are neighbors not just to their friends, to the people who live next door, to those who think and act like them, but to all people.

These good neighbors are moved with compassion when they see people in need. They not only empathize, but in mercy they reach out to help. Through these honorable people we see the story of the Good Samaritan told over and over again.

The lawyer asked Jesus "Who is my neighbor?" Perhaps our question should be, How can I be a neighbor? How can I show care?

There are little ways to serve, to lift the spirit of our neighbors. We can be cheerful even when our own problems are troublesome and all-absorbing. We can offer hospitality even when we feel shy and don't know what to say. We can listen to the troubled, and affirm the downhearted. We can help people believe in themselves.

Let us not spend so much time studying God's word that we never practice it; or so much time preaching his word that we never live it. Let us go and be honorable people doing honorable deeds, loving the Lord our God with all our heart and loving our neighbor as ourselves.

TALKING

1. Who is your neighbor? Talk about ways to be a good neighbor.

2. Discuss compassion, empathy and mercy. How do they differ? Name people who witness in each of these areas.

3. Share your answers:
   I show my love for God by _____.
   This week I will do this honorable deed: _____.
   I find it easy/hard to love my neighbor because _____.

DOING

1. Rank the following by how important you think they are to being a good neighbor.
being cheerful
being encouraging
showing understanding
spending time
visiting
being adaptable

2. Make your weekly scripture symbol—a hand with a heart inside. Place it in your home or on your SUNDAY THROUGHOUT THE YEAR banner.

PRAYING

Lord,
When we see someone in need, let us stop, place our wants, our needs, our tasks, our business aside, and be present to the needs of that person. Help us to become honorable people doing honorable deeds.

As a family, let us be good neighbors to one another.

Jul 10, 1983 / Jul 13, 1986 / Jul 16, 1989

16th Sunday of Ordinary Time (Lk 10:38-42)

REFLECTING

Mothers, fathers, sisters, brothers, cousins, aunts, uncles, grandparents. These people are a part of every family. How wonderful it is to belong and to help one another live a family life together.

God made a family visit to Abraham and Sarah in the guise of one of the three men in today's first reading (Gn 18:1-10). Abraham showed lavish hospitality in welcoming and feeding them. To Abraham and Sarah, the good news was announced that their family would soon increase with the birth of a son.

In today's gospel, we are presented with another family scene. Jesus visits the home of two sisters, Martha and Mary. Mary sat at the feet of Jesus, enthralled with his every word; Martha busied herself with all the details of hospitality. Anyone involved in preparing the household for entertaining, and anxious that everything possible be done to satisfy the needs of the guests knows what Martha felt when no one helped her. Everyone has experienced this feeling of doing all the work at some time in life.

Jesus' words to Martha shoud comfort us rather than bring grief. There is a time to serve through action and also a time for discipleship through prayer. Without spending time *listening* to the word of God in our lives, our actions would soon become empty and void of meaning. Without *doing* the word of God, we become hearers only, seeds bearing no fruit.

In both forms of service, we must first be intent on the Lord. He is our first priority. He *is* love of God and love of neighbor. And when we serve God we serve as Martha and Mary, for there is a little of both in each of us.

TALKING

1. How do you reconcile the need to live a life of both prayer and action?

2. Consider the Marthas and Marys in your own family. How do you each welcome God daily into your family?

3. Share your answers:
   I am most like Martha when I _____.
   I am most like Mary when I _____.
   I find it easy to serve God by _____; harder to serve him by _____.

DOING

1. Share the household responsibilities. Make a list of things to do in the home. Have family members place their name by the jobs they will do. Star jobs completed. Pray together as a family as you recognize and thank God for his presence in all your work.

2. Make your weekly scripture symbol—a sign of a family. Place it in your home or on your SUNDAY THROUGHOUT THE YEAR banner.

PRAYING

Lord,
We are Martha and Mary. Sometimes we become so busy with our work that we forget to think of you, to speak with you, to place you first in our life. Other times, we only want to sit and talk with you, listen to you, or be still in your presence. Sometimes we may hide in that presence and forget that in love, in your love, we must go forth and become busy loving your people. Thank you for a family that helps us to be both Martha and Mary in serving you. Amen.

Jul 17, 1983 / Jul 20, 1986 / Jul 23, 1989

CYCLE C

17th Sunday of Ordinary Time (Lk 11:1-13)

REFLECTING

"Prayer enlarges the heart until it is capable of containing God's gift of himself." These words spoken by Mother Teresa of Calcutta reflect the way she lives her life. At 4:30 a.m. she begins her day with prayer. "Love to pray. Feel during the day the need to pray and take trouble to pray."

The apostles also felt a deep need to pray. Curious from watching Jesus pray, they asked if he would teach them. It was the prayer of petition that Jesus taught. We can hardly claim to have been taught to pray by Christ himself if we have not learned this practice of petitionary prayer.

It is because of our friendship with God that we know we can rely on him in times of need. In today's gospel, Jesus makes it clear that God is a loving parent who understands our needs and wants to give us, his children, all that we ask for. Like Abraham, we are confident that God is our trusting friend and that he cares for us. And like Abraham we should entreat God to answer our requests. Ask over and over. Knock again and again. We will be answered; the door will be opened, sometimes in ways we least expect.

In teaching us to pray, Jesus offers the Our Father. In this prayer we have an opening address to God, a praise of God, and a conclusion asking for help. During the fifth century a benediction which praises God's greatness was added.

Let us love to pray, and pray always until our hearts enlarge to hold the gift of God himself.

TALKING

1. Describe an experience of prayer answered in an unexpected way.

2. Imagine Jesus saying to you, "Ask and you will receive." Do you really believe these words? What do they mean to you?

3. Share your answers:
   My most persistent prayer is _____.
   A situation in which I needed to pray was _____.
   The part of the Our Father that speaks to me deeply right now is

   _____.

DOING

1. Write a family prayer based on the Our Father. Place a sheet of paper on your refrigerator with the heading: Lord, we ask help for _____. Write the name of people and situations of need. As a family, pray this prayer of petition daily.

2. Make your weekly scripture symbol—the word "Ask." Place it in your home or on your SUNDAY THROUGHOUT THE YEAR banner.

PRAYING

God,
You are our Father. We are your children. Your name is holy to us. Help us to do your will in all things.
Give us, Lord, bread to strengthen us every day of our life; give us the bread of your life to live forever.
Forgive us and guide us to walk your way.
We lift up our hands as we praise you with this benediction: For yours is the kingdom and the power and the glory now and for ever. Amen.

Jul 24, 1983 / Jul 27, 1986 / Jul 30, 1989

18th Sunday of Ordinary Time (Lk 12:13-21)

REFLECTING

In a poignant scene from *Zorba the Greek*, we hear the wailing of the professional mourners, and we see the greed of the relatives as they clear the death room of every belonging and possession of the dead woman. We are shocked by the callousness of this scene.

In response, we could echo the words of the preacher in today's first reading (Eccl 1:2, 2:21-23): "All things are vanity." One works hard and accumulates possessions only to die and have others inherit them or fight over them. In today's gospel we encounter the brother who petitions Jesus to arbitrate a family will in his favor.

Greed and meanness are common human failings; we meet them not only in the business world but also in family life. Greed divides families. Disputes about money destroy family relationships.

Jesus gave us a concrete warning of what happens to one who is preoccupied with amassing wealth. In this parable, a rich man longs for security, for a retirement plan of grain in his bins which will support him for years to come. But where will his piled-up wealth go when he dies? He is a fool to waste his time growing rich, when it should be spent responding to the call of God.

We should be on our guard. Our reasonable desire to have security can easily become greed to have and own at the expense of others and at the risk of failing to grow rich in the sight of God.

TALKING

1. Discuss wills, savings, retirement and insurance plans. What are the possible advantages and disadvantages of them?

2. As a family, talk about ways to heal broken relationships that come from greed or money disputes. If needed, plan a reconciliation.

3. Share your answers:
   To detach myself from things, I will _____.
   My safeguard in avoiding greed is _____.
   I am like the rich fool when I _____.

DOING

1. As a family, design, write, and post a will that leaves all things to God.

2. Make your weekly scripture symbol—a silo. Place it in your home or on your SUNDAY THROUGHOUT THE YEAR banner.

PRAYING

Lord,

I am the foolish rich man for I sometimes place my trust in worldly possessions. I foolishly think that the clothes I wear, the car and home I own, the things I possess define me; that they are me. I have argued over expenses and been preoccupied with money and savings. While I own the things that are necessary for my well being, let me never become attached to them. Let me always be intent on one thing: listening and responding to your presence in my life.

(Turn to one another and ask forgiveness for the times you have been greedy at the expense of another.)

Jul 31, 1983 / Aug 3, 1986

CYCLE C

19th Sunday of Ordinary Time (Lk 12:32-48)

REFLECTING

Many people had tried to walk through the labyrinth, to pass the test, and to gain the treasure. All had lost their way and failed to return. The maze was too difficult. One day a young man decided to unravel a ball of string as he walked. The string would guide him safely out of the maze.

This myth from Joseph Campbell's *Hero With a Thousand Faces* speaks clearly of a task that each of us must accomplish: to go forth, to do something, and to return home again. The journey can be a frightening one but we have before us men and women who have walked the labyrinth of life and have left their footprints for us to follow.

In the story of Abraham and Sarah in our second reading (Heb 11:1-2, 8-19) we have our heroes and their footprints to follow. With faith, Abraham journeyed to a strange land. By faith, Sarah conceived a child. In faith, Abraham met the test and willingly offered his son to be sacrificed. Because of their faith, their descendents were as numerous as the stars in the sky and the sands of the seashore.

The journey of life can only be walked in faith. The foundation of that faith is a deep trust in the things we cannot see, a profound hope in things yet to be, and a confident assurance that we will return home again.

Jesus is our model of faithfulness and endurance. He has walked the labyrinth of life and has promised us that we need never take that journey alone. He will walk with us and he will bring us home.

TALKING

1. Many stories speak of going out, doing something, and returning home. Have family members share fairy tales built around this theme.

2. Talk about the journey of Abraham and Sarah—their fears, hopes, dreams, the sacrifices they made. Relate a similar experience you have had as a family.

3. Share your answers:
   For me, this faith journey seems _____.
   Faith is _____.
   To return home is to _____.

DOING

1. On poster paper, chart your faith journey as a family (moments of disappointment, questioning, forgiveness, love, homecomings ...).

2. Make your weekly scripture symbol—sand and stars. Place the symbol in your home or on your SUNDAY THROUGHOUT THE YEAR banner.

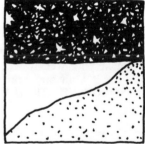

PRAYING

Lord,
We long to be at home with you. This journey of faith is hard. Sometimes we lose our way, become tired and discouraged, forget to place our trust in you. Many times the faith road is frightening and lonely.

We thank you for the men and women who have walked before us and showed us a way. We thank you for the sacrifice you made as you showed us how to journey home to your Father.

Come, Lord, and walk with us. Amen.

Aug 7, 1983 / Aug 10, 1986 / Aug 13, 1989

20th Sunday of Ordinary Time (Lk 12:49-53)

REFLECTING

When her carriage became stuck deep in mud, Teresa of Avila complained to God, "If this is how you treat your friends, it's no wonder you have so few of them."

The prophet Jeremiah could have shared this same lament. Chosen by God at a young age to be a prophet, Jeremiah preached for 40 years through the reign of five kings. During this time, he was continually insulted and ridiculed by the people, beaten, reprimanded by the priests and king, arrested and sent to prison.

On one occasion, as revealed in our first reading (Jer 38:4-6, 8-10), the princes of the court threw Jeremiah into a waterless cistern. He sank deep in the mud. Convinced that he would die without food, an Ethiopian received permission from the king to rescue Jeremiah.

But who could rescue Jeremiah from his frustration in preaching to a people who refused to listen? In their hard and stubborn hearts the people continued to place their trust in wealth and power and not in God. And who could help Jeremiah with his doubts? As a man of truth Jeremiah was plagued with the possibility that he was a false prophet as the people professed. Continuously he prayed and received from God signs that he was doing God's will.

Like Jeremiah, we sometimes feel crushed and abandoned, ridiculed and rejected by others. We, too, wonder how God could allow us, his friends, to be treated in such a way. But God's ways are not our ways. Let us be faithful like Jeremiah to God's call and have heart; God's friendship covenant will be with us forever.

TALKING

1. Traditional prophets foretold doom for people who disobeyed the word of God. False prophets told only of peace and good times and placed no burdens on the people to do God's will. How do you know and avoid false prophets today?

2. Identify and share events in your life when you experienced feelings and thoughts similar to those of Jeremiah. Talk about Jeremiah's constant faithfulness in doing God's will.

3. Share your answers:
   When I am ridiculed, I _____.
   When I fail, I _____.
   I feel I am in a muddy well when _____.

DOING

1. Encourage someone who is discouraged by a phone call, a note or a visit.

2. Make your weekly scripture symbol—a well. Place it in your home or on your SUNDAY THROUGHOUT THE YEAR banner.

PRAYING

Lord,
You sent your prophets to remind us to be your faithful people. Help us to understand your word written deep inside your hearts. Let us welcome people who speak in your name and be ever ready to rescue them from the muddy wells the world sometimes makes for them.

Treat us always as your friends. We are many in your name. Amen.

Aug 14, 1983 / Aug 17, 1986 / Aug 20, 1989

CYCLE C

21st Sunday of Ordinary Time (Lk 13:22-30)

REFLECTING

There is a story that has become part of the tradition of many countries. In the Korean version the story goes like this: A child asked the storyteller what heaven and hell are like. The storyteller replied: "Picture a long table filled with wondrous delights. The people come, sit down, and eagerly pick up their chopsticks for this feast. See their frustrations as they try to eat with three-foot chopsticks. If this is what hell is like, picture now a scene from heaven. There is a long table filled with wondrous delights." The child excitedly interrupted the story: "Oh, I know, honorable storyteller. These people have short chopsticks." And then she proudly concluded, "That is the difference between heaven and hell." The storyteller smiled. "No, my child, these people in heaven also have three-foot chopsticks . . . only here the people feed one another."

In today's gospel Jesus speaks of the people who will feast in the kingdom of God: Abraham, Isaac, Jacob, the prophets, people from north, south, east and west, all people who have faithfully walked the road to Jerusalem with Jesus. They will knock at the door and Jesus will recognize them.

In order to journey with Jesus on this faith road, to be recognized by him, it is not enough to simply listen to his words and to eat and drink with him. To be followers we must *do* his word and *live* his life. We must make a personal commitment to him.

Jesus invites the entire world to follow him. In response to the prophecy of Isaiah in our first reading (Is 66:18-21), we are to go to the four corners of the earth to proclaim God's glory. It will take a lifetime of hard work. But we can overcome any difficulty, for through Christ we know how to prepare to eat the feast of the kingdom.

TALKING

1. Talk about the four marks of the church: one, holy, Catholic and apostolic.

2. Share specific ways you can feed one another in preparation for the feast of the kingdom.

3. Share your answers:
   I will bring God's word to _____.
   To become a doer, I will _____.
   For me, the kingdom is like _____.

DOING

1. Become a storyteller and in story form explain the feast of the kingdom. Design and display an invitation to this feast. Have family members R.S.V.P. by signing the invitation.

2. Make your weekly scripture symbol—a feast table. Place it in your home or on your SUNDAY THROUGHOUT THE YEAR banner.

PRAYING

Response: We go out to all the world and live your life.

Lord,
After we eat and drink with you . . .
After we listen to your word . . .
After we proclaim your glory . . .
After we walk to Jerusalem with you . . .

We accept your invitation, Lord, to the feast of the kingdom. You will recognize us when we come to your door and knock, for we will remain faithful to your word. As your family, help us to live for others. Amen.

Aug 21, 1983 / Aug 24, 1986 / Aug 27, 1989

22nd Sunday of Ordinary Time (Lk 14:1, 7-14)

REFLECTING

> In the twilight of life, God will not judge us on our earthly possessions
> and human success, but rather on how much we have loved.
> —St. John of the Cross

In today's gospel, we discover that God is not impressed with our social standing, with the number of times we have dined at the homes of the socially prominent, the cultured, the wealthy. Nor does he rejoice when our guest list includes only those people who have invited us to their homes. Instead, he asks us to invite people who cannot repay us.

Practicing this social etiquette of Jesus is difficult. We have grown up with the cliche: Tell me who you go with and I'll tell you who you are. Could this be so deeply engrained that we are ashamed to be seen with the unfortunate, the illiterate, for fear that people will think us the same?

Not only does Jesus challenge our motivation in inviting people to our homes, but he explains the modest behavior that should be ours while dining with others. While at the table of a Pharisee, Jesus observed the guests as they vied for the seat of honor. In parable form, he spoke of choosing the lowest place.

How comfortable we feel with people who are humble, who do not laud their accomplishments and position in life over us. It is to the humble that God's blessings are given. It is in the twilight of life that the humble are rewarded for how much they have loved and lived with a proper estimation of their own worth and the worth of others.

TALKING

1. Recall invitations you have accepted. How do you repay your host or hostess? What are your feelings when you are not invited to a party and your friends are?
2. Talk about modest behavior in all that you do.
3. Share your answers:
   For Jesus to eat at the home of a Pharisee was _____.
   To be humble is _____.
   I show my love for the poor, the handicapped, the unfortunate by
   _____.

DOING

1. List the social manners you should have when eating any meal. Plan to invite someone for dinner who cannot repay you.

2. Make your weekly scripture symbol—a guest list. Place it in your home or on your SUNDAY THROUGHOUT THE YEAR banner.

PRAYING

Lord,
We welcome all people into our home for they are your people. We invite them to eat with us. We bow our heads for your blessing upon us, upon all people who love.

Leader: May we receive the peace of God.
All: Amen.

Leader: May we know his joy.
All: Amen.

Leader: May we live his humility.
All: Amen.

Aug 28, 1983 / Aug 31, 1986 / Sep 3, 1989

CYCLE C

23rd Sunday of Ordinary Time (Lk 14:25-33)

REFLECTING

In his book, *Man's Search for Meaning*, Viktor Frankl shares the story of his life in a concentration camp during World War II. Through these experiences, Frankl lived and confirmed his hypothesis that our will to meaning is one of our strongest drives and that we are called in freedom to choose our attitude in a given set of circumstances. Frankl contends that if we have a *why*, a task and a goal, then we can bear any *how*, any situation, any environment, for the realization of this goal.

Like Frankl, the author of the Wisdom literature is concerned with the spiritual issues of our existence. In our first reading (Wis 9:13-18) this writer uses Solomon, a man of wisdom who prayed to God for an understanding heart, to speak his prayer. It is only with the wisdom of an understanding heart that we can know what is pleasing to God and live his will in our lives.

Wisdom is identified with the Spirit of the Lord; it is God's Holy Spirit sent from on high. Wisdom is a gift of the Holy Spirit, a gift which helps us to see clearly, to judge all the events in our lives according to our belief in God, to see life as a remarkable gift from God. During the rite of confirmation we pray that God will send the Holy Spirit to us as a helper and guide and give us the spirit of wisdom. With one of the O Antiphons, we pray: "O Wisdom, who came from the mouth of the Most High, who reaches from end to end, who gives order to all things mightily and sweetly, come to us."

It is only in wisdom that our search for meaning can be realized. Like the Wisdom writer, let us be fascinated with Solomon who sought only for a heart to understand the ways of God. May we pray daily for the Holy Spirit from on high to give wisdom, direction and meaning to our lives.

TALKING

1. Talk about the gifts of wisdom.

2. Do you think your basic drive is for pleasure (Freud), power (Adler) or meaning (Frankl)? Share ways you find and bring meaning to your life.

3. Share your answers:
   With an understanding heart, I can _____.
   My search for meaning is _____.
   With wisdom I can _____.

DOING

1. Make bookmarks. On one side of a strip of cardboard write a prayer for wisdom. Design and place signs for wisdom on the reverse side.

2. Make your weekly scripture symbol—a bird to represent wisdom. Place it in your home or on your SUNDAY THROUGHOUT THE YEAR banner.

PRAYING

(For the beginning of school, parents or teachers read this prayer while placing their hands over the heads of the children.)

Lord,
Send them your wisdom as they begin the school year. Give them the joy of a new beginning and the excitement of learning and discovering new things.

Be with them as they meet their friends. Help them to grow in understanding your word and your people.

(*Name*), go forth with the wisdom of the Spirit of God to learn.

24th Sunday of Ordinary Time (Lk 15:1-32)

REFLECTING

One sacred memory from childhood is the best education.

—Dostoyevsky

Memories enrich our lives. Sometimes a memory presents itself when we least expect it. Memories that have touched our life can sustain us through difficult times. Sometimes these experiences are stored inside us as though in cold storage. They incubate and emerge years later.

In our gospel story today, it was the remembrance of his father's goodness that encouraged the lost son to risk a return home. In a sense, we could say that the father began seeking the son by means of this memory even before the boy made his decision to return home. The experience of the goodness of the father needed time to incubate. We rejoice that there was this sacred memory from childhood that called forth a homecoming.

Jesus seeks each of us through our memories of his goodness and then rejoices when we are found. A woman cautiously sweeps her home hoping to hear the tinkle of her lost coin against the floor. A shepherd searches for one lost sheep. When lost and separated from the flock, sheep will lie down and refuse to move. Shepherds must carry the sheep on their shoulders, sometimes for long distances. Jesus searches for the lost coin and the lost sheep. People who are lost, sinners, come to Jesus because he goes first to them.

Luke emphasizes the joy in finding that which was lost. A party was given for the lost son; friends and neighbors were invited by the woman and the shepherd to celebrate and rejoice in their good fortune. God calls us to rejoice with him always over the finding and return of that which was lost. Good memories can help us return home to God and to one another.

TALKING

1. Recall people from your childhood that you admired. Share your memory of their goodness. Share your memory experiences of God's goodness.

2. Talk about the experience of joy that comes from searching and finding. How and with whom do you share this joy?

3. Share your answers:

I am like the lost son when I _____.

One treasured memory from my childhood is _____.

DOING

1. As a family, pantomime one of the joy stories from today's gospel. Make and display signs of rejoicing. Have a family party to celebrate the return of the lost son, the lost coin, or the lost sheep—and your own homecoming.

2. Make your weekly scripture symbol—the word "Joy." Place it in your home or on your SUNDAY THROUGHOUT THE YEAR banner.

PRAYING

God our Father,

You show mercy to all of us who have turned away from you and then returned home to you. You rejoice and celebrate our homecoming.

Help me to treasure those memories of your goodness through the people in my life. Let those memories call me home when I am lost. And let me experience that deep inside joy that must be shared with others.

Sep 11, 1983 / Sep 17, 1989

CYCLE C

25th Sunday of Ordinary Time (Lk 16:1-13)

REFLECTING

We enjoyed and marveled at the cleverness of the two con artists in the movie, *The Sting*. Not until the surprise ending did we fully understand that we had been fooled ourselves.

Today's gospel tells what happens when people try to use their wealth and position to gain God's favor. A rich man calls his manager for an accounting. The manager knows he may lose his job. So, to win the friendship of his master's debtors, he requires only the principal owed to satisfy his employer. The employer admires his manager's cleverness and self-interest.

In today's first reading (Am 8:4-7), the prophet Amos speaks powerfully against the greed and self-interest of his day. He warns those who cheat the poor with their clever practices.

Amos was the prophetic voice who called for humane and just conditions of life for all people. In some ways the world hasn't changed much since his day. It is still divided between the "haves" and "have nots."

Like Amos, we too are called to be prophets for justice. We must become committed to social justice for all people. We cannot continue to applaud the shrewd and clever practices of political or economic systems which take advantage of the poor for their own growth. Reflecting on the words of scripture, let us reach out to the victims of injustice and work for peace and justice for all.

TALKING

1. Discuss ways you can become involved in working for peace and justice.

2. Talk about clever practices in which you have been the victim. How do you avoid using money and position to gain friendships?

3. Share your answers:
   If I were the manager, I would have _____.
   For me, the rich man is _____.
   To begin to help the poor, I will _____.

DOING

1. Find newspaper articles and pictures that tell of the poor. Cut them out and make a poster. Write boldly across the poster, "We will help."

2. Make your weekly scripture symbol—coins. Place the symbol in your home or on your SUNDAY THROUGHOUT THE YEAR banner.

PRAYING

(In the second reading (1 Tm 2:1-8) Paul asks us to pray for others. Write your petitions and pray them as a family.)

Response: Lord, hear our prayer.

_____, let us pray to the Lord ...
_____, let us pray to the Lord ...
_____, let us pray to the Lord ...

Sep 18, 1983 / Sep 21, 1986 / Sep 24, 1989

26th Sunday of Ordinary Time (Lk 16:19-31)

REFLECTING

> Is not this the sort of fast that pleases me ...
> to share your bread with the hungry,
> and shelter the homeless poor,
> to clothe the man you see to be naked
> and not turn from your own kin?
>
> —*Isaiah 58:7*

Jesus lived his life among the poor. He taught that we will be happy only if we live the life of the beatitudes. In today's gospel the concerned rich man was told that his five brothers had adequate and clear signs from Abraham, Moses and the prophets, that they should give up their self-centered life of money and riches. They do not need the return of the beggar Lazarus to convince them.

The Pharisees believed that riches are a proof of God's approval of a person's way of life. How shattering for them to hear this story of the rich man tormented in the after-life and the consoled beggar Lazarus resting happily with Abraham after his death.

Wealth can bring us a false sense of security, a security that makes us turn away from God and forget our dependence upon him. It is not wrong to have riches as long as we share and use them to answer the needs of the hungry, the naked and the homeless.

TALKING

1. Imagine walking one day in the shoes of the poor. How different would life be for you?

2. Sometimes we become envious of the wealthy, even those who share their wealth with others. Discuss ways to accept the good fortune of others and to become joyful over their accomplishments and their generosity.

3. Share your answers:
   For me, making money is _____.
   My attitude toward the poor is _____.
   If I were one of the five brothers, I would _____.

DOING

1. Plan this month to refurbish worn clothes and mend broken things. Try to develop an attitude of fixing and recycling what the family already owns. Have one meal of rice or barley. Send the remaining money alloted for that meal to a relief service.

2. Make your weekly scripture symbol—a tattered cloak. Place it in your home or on your SUNDAY THROUGHOUT THE YEAR banner.

PRAYING

Response: Lord, we have heard and will do your word.

Lord,
May we become aware of the poor and sensitive to their needs ...
May we "share your bread with the hungry" ...
May we "shelter the homeless poor" ...
May we "clothe the man" we see to be naked ...
May we "not turn" from our own kin ...

Lord,
May we never become hardened by the culture in which we live. Help us, Lord, never to be afraid to see and to touch those who are in need. Amen.

Sep 25, 1983 / Sep 28, 1986 / Oct 1, 1989

27th Sunday of Ordinary Time (Lk 17:5-10)

REFLECTING

> Dear Grandma,
> I heard you are sick. I hope you get well soon. I will say a prayer for
> you.
>
> Love,
Willie

How beautiful it is to receive a note from someone you love! It is also refreshing to receive a letter of encouragement that affirms you as a person and supports the work you are doing.

Though Paul was alone, in prison, and aware of his approaching death, he continued to think of others. He wrote a letter of encouragement to Timothy, a young and shy bishop who was ill and discouraged: "God's gift was not a spirit of timidity, but the Spirit of power, and love, and self-control" (2 Tm 1:7). Like Timothy, we need to have our faith enlivened daily through the Spirit so we will have the courage to do God's work.

The sacrament of holy orders gives the Spirit and confers spiritual powers through the laying on of hands. Through the sacrament Timothy had received "God's gift" to preach. Paul encouraged Timothy to trust that same Spirit.

We must not just timidly guard our faith as a family inheritance or gift wrap it and hide it in a closet for safekeeping. Together let us reawaken our faith daily with the help of the Holy Spirit who lives with us.

TALKING

1. In what ways could you increase your faith as a family?

2. Discuss your feelings and your response to a person with a strong and energetic personality like Paul's. If you have this type of personality, how do you feel about your interactions with others?

3. Share your answers:
   When I am shy like Timothy, I _____.
   I offer encouragement to others by _____.

DOING

1. We should pray daily not just for health and prosperity but for an increase in our faith. As a family, write a morning prayer and say it daily.

2. Make your weekly scripture symbol—a letter. Place it in your home or on your SUNDAY THROUGHOUT THE YEAR banner.

PRAYING

Dear God,
It takes faith to work day in and day out. Through baptism we know we are your children and have received your gift of faith. Never let us take our faith for granted. Let us encourage and support each family member as a special and unique person of faith. Lord, as a family, increase our faith in you and in one another.

(Place your hand on each family member's shoulder in turn and say: (*Name*), keep up the good work you are doing in _____.)

28th Sunday of Ordinary Time (Lk 17:11-19)

REFLECTING

> Praise the Lord all you people on this earth,
> Thank him kindly for the moment of your birth,
> Praise the Lord for his kingdom now has come,
> Shining brightly, the brilliance of the sun.
>
> —*Apple*,
> a film from Ikonographics

How often we forget to praise God in our lives! Sometimes we act like the nine lepers—ungrateful, unappreciative, forgetting that it is only through Jesus that God chooses to heal us.

Realizing that he had been cured, the 10th leper, the Samaritan, came back praising God in a loud voice. Only this one leper saw clearly that his healing was due to Jesus and that through faith in Jesus he could be saved.

The people understood that leprosy could only be cured by a special act of God. So too sin can only be forgiven by a special act of God. This foreigner understood Jesus' role as the bringer of God's love and mercy to those in need, whether physical or spiritual.

Only when we humbly turn to God and praise his presence in Jesus will we be cured. Only then will we begin our journey into freedom, freedom from our self-centeredness, freedom to live for God and his people.

TALKING

1. People are sometimes embarrassed about offering or receiving praise. How often and in what ways do you give and receive compliments?

2. Talk about the times you have returned to give thanks or show gratitude to someone for what he or she has done for you.

3. Share your answers:
   When I am praised I feel _____.
   I am like the leper who returned when I _____.
   I am like the ungrateful leper when I _____.

DOING

1. As a family, take a praise walk through the woods. Praise God for what you see and hear. Place an autumn sign of God's creation on the supper table. Have family members write notes of appreciation and praise to one another.

2. Make your weekly scripture symbol—a figure with a smiling face and arms extended upward. Place it in your home or on your SUNDAY THROUGHOUT THE YEAR banner.

PRAYING

(Extend hands with palms up for each response.)
Response: Praise the Lord.
For the flowers, waterfalls, and trees ...
For sunlight and colored autumn leaves ...
For birthdays ...
For friends, mothers and fathers, sisters and brothers ...
(Add your own special thanksgivings.)

For all that you have made, for loving us, for always being in our life, we praise you, God! Alleluia! Alleluia!

Oct 9, 1983 / Oct 12, 1986 / Oct 15, 1989

CYCLE C

29th Sunday of Ordinary Time (Lk 18:1-8)

REFLECTING

I fled Him, down the nights and down the days;
I fled Him, down the arches of the years ...
That Voice is round me like a bursting sea:
Whom wilt thou find to love ignoble thee,
Save Me, save only Me?

—Francis Thompson
The Hound of Heaven

Just as God persistently pursues and hounds the man wherever he goes in Thompson's poem, so we, through our constant faith and steady love, pursue God. We become like the widow, determined and relentless as we call upon God. If the judge finally listens to her repeated requests, how much more will God listen to us, the people whom he loves.

In today's gospel, Jesus again speaks on prayer. In this parable, he teaches us to pray always for God's final coming and never lose heart. Many of the disciples were afraid that Jesus would not return. We know that *when* he comes doesn't matter as long as we have remained faithful in our daily friendship with him.

It is easy to become excited and committed to a new venture, but it is often difficult to persevere in that original commitment. Let us be constant in our walk with God, and daily recommit ourselves to him. May we pray always and never lose heart.

TALKING

1. Talk about different commitments you have made, for example, to scouting, sports, a musical instrument, doing well in a class or work. How do you recommit yourself when you begin to lose enthusiasm?

2. Discuss ways to pray throughout your day, not only for help, but in the very actions you are doing.

3. Share your answers:
   I find it easy/hard to pray when _____.
   I am like the widow when _____.
   When I lose heart, I _____.

DOING

1. Write a recommitment of love and faith to God on a scroll. Have each family member sign it. Proclaim your recommitment together as a prayer before mealtime.

2. Make your weekly scripture symbol—hands in prayer. Place the symbol in your home or on your SUNDAY THROUGHOUT THE YEAR banner.

PRAYING

Lord, teach me to be generous;
teach me to serve you as you deserve;
to give and not to count the cost,
to fight and not to heed the wounds,
to toil and not to seek for rest,
to labor and to ask for no reward,
save that of knowing I am doing your will. Amen.

—Prayer of St. Ignatius Loyola

Oct 16, 1983 / Oct 19, 1986 / Oct 22, 1989

30th Sunday of Ordinary Time (Lk: 18:9-14)

REFLECTING

"I can run faster than you."

"I get the highest grades in my class."

"I can play ball better than anyone on the team."

Sometimes we put down other people in order to make ourselves look important.

In today's gospel, the Pharisee compared himself to others and offered a prayer of thanksgiving to God that he was not like everybody else. Perhaps our prayer should be one of thanksgiving that we are like others. Like others, we depend upon God for our very existence. With others, we share the human condition, a condition capable of love, a condition always in need of forgiveness. Because we see ourselves in others, we can be understanding of one another.

The publican, because of his occupation as a tax collector and his companionship with people who were not his own, lived alone. He was rejected by the Pharisees who believed in total separation from the Gentiles. Though alone, with no one to remind him of his relationship with God, his prayer at the temple was the humble prayer of total dependence on God.

How much we can learn from this parable. We should never compare ourselves to others or exalt ourselves over others, but instead recognize and rejoice that we are like one another in our need of God.

TALKING

1. Though we are unique persons, in what ways are we like others? Henri J. M. Nouwen in *Reaching Out* rejoices that he is like other men and women. How does this make you feel?

2. How can we become more aware of our total dependence upon God, aware that we owe God everything?

3. Share your answers:
I am most like the publican/Pharisee when _____.
When someone boasts, I _____.
When I try to look important, I _____.

DOING

1. Be like the Pharisee and list all you do. Be like the publican and write with your family a prayer of humble thanksgiving.

2. Make your weekly scripture symbol—a temple. Place it in your home or on your SUNDAY THROUGHOUT THE YEAR banner.

PRAYING

Lord,
We want to grow as a family in loving you and in loving one another. Together we reflect and pray:
Do I love myself as God loves me? (Pause)
Do I exalt myself before others? (Pause)
Am I humble and do I have a proper estimation of myself? (Pause)
Do I rejoice that I am like others in my need to be loved and forgiven? (Pause)

As a sign of our growth and oneness as a family, we hold hands and say the Our Father together. Our Father, . . .

Oct 23, 1983 / Oct 26, 1986 / Oct 29, 1989

CYCLE C

31st Sunday of Ordinary Time (Lk 19:1-10)

REFLECTING

Talk shows in which famous people are interviewed have become popular on radio and television. We are curious and want to know why someone has chosen to live a particular lifestyle. Through questions and answers, people reveal themselves to us.

Picture an interviewer asking this question of a man who lived during the time of Christ: "Could you please tell the audience how you were able to find this new way of life and what prompted you to choose it?"

As we listen to the man's reply, let us see if we recognize his identity.

"It was hard at first to live this new way. You see, I am very wealthy. Life was easy. I simply took from others in order to make a profit for myself. But one day ... well ... let me tell you the story from the beginning. I had become very curious about Jesus, a man who was preaching in the village. I wanted to see him, but I couldn't see through the crowd. So I climbed a tree and waited for him to speak. Well, Jesus saw me as he walked by. He stopped, looked up, called my name, and told me to go home and prepare a meal. He wanted to have dinner at my home.

"You can imagine my amazement! Me! My house! This man Jesus coming to my table! The people were shocked. You see, as their chief tax collector I was not the most popular figure in our village.

"Well, that night during supper, with Jesus, I became a changed man. I promised to give half my money to the poor and if I had ever defrauded anyone to pay that person back fourfold. If you had been there, you would have done the same.

"I've stopped worrying about getting money and keeping it; I've become less concerned about myself and more concerned about others. I'm finding new life by following the man Jesus."

"Thank you, Zacchaeus; and now for our next interview."

TALKING

1. Jesus came for all people, even sinners and those rejected by society. Talk about the way Zacchaeus changed. List ways we can become less concerned with ourselves and more concerned with others.

2. Share your answers:
   I would like to interview (*Name*) and ask _____.
   I find it easy/hard to change to a new way of life because _____.

DOING

1. Write an invitation to Jesus to come to your home. Post the invitation on a door in your home.

2. Make your weekly scripture symbol—the outline of a man by a tree. Place it in your home or on your SUNDAY THROUGHOUT THE YEAR banner.

PRAYING

Jesus,
You came to offer a new way of life. You were always more concerned with others than with yourself. Help us to become like you. May we be willing to change as Zacchaeus did. May we always be ready to rejoice as we welcome you, Jesus, into our homes and our hearts. Amen.

Oct 30, 1983 / Nov 5, 1989

32nd Sunday of Ordinary Time (Lk 20:27-38)

REFLECTING

On the plains, on the mountainside, in the country, Jesus spoke. In towns, by lakes, along the sea, Jesus touched the people with his words. By meadows, along the roads, at the markets, the people listened to the words of Jesus.

It was in the Temple that Jesus' words were constantly challenged by the Jewish leaders. Jesus as a teacher was welcome to speak at the Temple, but the Sadducees did not accept what he was saying and began to ridicule him before the people.

The Sadducees accepted only the five books of Moses as the word of God. Here they found no mention of life after death. They taunted and tried to trick Jesus when he taught about life after death.

In today's gospel some of the Sadducees pose the problem of the wife and the seven brothers. Jesus affirmed the resurrection of the body and called those who have died "children of the resurrection . . . sons of God." And he says about God that "he is God, not of the dead, but of the living; for to him all men are in fact alive."

Our resurrection is a gift of God to us. How wonderful to have such a gift, the gift of being able to live forever with God.

TALKING

1. To understand death in a Christian way is to see death as a change in—not an end of—life. Discuss.

2. Because of Jesus' resurrection, we will rise to new life. Talk about the resurrection of the body.

3. Share your answers:
    For the gift of the resurrection, I say _____.
    I am like the Sadducees when I _____.

DOING

1. Make small signs that say, "I believe in the resurrection of the body and life everlasting." Place a sign on every mirror in your home.

2. Make your weekly scripture symbol—a resurrection cross. Place it in your home or on your SUNDAY THROUGHOUT THE YEAR banner.

PRAYING

Response: We believe in the resurrection of the body and life everlasting.
Sometimes we become discouraged and forget that . . .
Sometimes we have doubts and fail to remember that . . .
Sometimes we are afraid and life seems to hold little meaning and we recall that . . .

Thank you, God, for this gift of life and the promise of a never-ending life with you. Help us to live now as sons and daughters of the resurrection, fully alive to your life within us. Amen.

CYCLE C

33rd Sunday of Ordinary Time (Lk 21:5-19)

REFLECTING

> You know how you ought to imitate us. . . . we worked day and night, laboring to the point of exhaustion so as not to impose on any of you... anyone who would not work should not eat ... some of you are unruly, not keeping busy but acting like busybodies.
> —*2 Thessalonians 3:7-11, NAB*

How clearly Paul speaks to the Thessalonian people in today's second reading (2 Thes 3:7-12). The community is confused about the Second Coming of Jesus, awaiting this coming in idleness, not knowing what to do. The people live an undemanding manner of life and are not willing to work. Paul challenges them to follow his example, "We worked night and day." This is the way to wait for the coming of Jesus.

Paul worked for a living; his trade was probably tent making. It is clear that Paul never wished to impose on any of the churches for personal financial assistance.

Our work can bring us joy, the feeling of accomplishment for a job well done. Our work can be done, not for the money we receive, but for the responsibility we have to build the earth, to make this old world into a new one.

As a family, we await the Second Coming of Christ by doing our work peacefully and quietly and by avoiding "keeping busy like busybodies."

TALKING

1. There are 122 occupations mentioned in the bible. Today over 22,000 areas of work are available to those who qualify. Talk about some of these occupations. Consider what happens to people who are unable to get a job and are deprived of the pride one can get from work.

2. Imagine and describe the happenings that prompted Paul to write this epistle to the Thessalonians. In what way could we apply these words to our world today?

3. Share your answers:
   I am a busybody when I _____.
   I feel _____ when I help around my home.
   I feel _____ when I sit around all day and do nothing.

DOING

1. List the words and feelings that come to mind when you hear the word "work."

2. Make your weekly scripture symbol—a sign with the words, "Work hard." Place it in your home or on your SUNDAY THROUGHOUT THE YEAR banner.

PRAYING

Dear Holy Spirit,
You are with us in the work we do to build the earth. May we never be afraid of hard work. Direct us to the occupations that will use our gifts best. Guide us to help all people find work and have dignity and joy in that work. Be with us as we wait together for the Second Coming of Jesus. Amen.

Solemnity of Christ the King (Lk 23:35-43)

REFLECTING

> As king he claims dominion over all creation,
> that he may present to you, his almighty Father,
> an eternal and universal kingdom:
> a kingdom of truth and life,
> a kingdom of holiness and grace,
> a kingdom of justice, love, and peace.
>
> —from the Preface of the Mass of Christ the King

Our liturgical year ends with this celebration of the feast of Christ the King. In this mystery we proclaim the reign of Jesus over all of creation. He came to share and live his life with us. Through his death we are able to live life forever with him.

The mocking inscription, *This is the king of the Jews*, was placed over the cross of Jesus. How little did the people realize the truth of this proclamation. We echo the words of the thief at his right side, "Jesus, remember me when you come into your kingdom."

The kingdom of Jesus has already begun, and we have been welcomed to share it with him. We have been asked to work for the fulfillment of this kingdom. When we live in truth, in holiness, in justice and in peace, we know we are already living the life of the kingdom. When we live the life of the beatitudes we become light that guides and salt that flavors the kingdom.

TALKING

1. Talk about the beatitudes which tell how to live the life of the kingdom. What does it mean to say that his kingdom has already begun but is not yet fulfilled?
2. How do you become a sign of the kingdom to others? Talk about ways to live in truth, holiness, justice, love and peace.

DOING

1. Make a crown from a circle of paper. On it write "This is the king of the Jews." Use it for Praying (see below) and as a centerpiece for the week. Draw smaller crowns and place them on the doors in your home during the procession (see Praying, below) as a sign of your family's willingness to recognize and accept Jesus as king over all creation.
2. Make your weekly scripture symbol—a crown. Place it in your home or on your SUNDAY THROUGHOUT THE YEAR banner.

PRAYING

(Hold the crown on high as the family proclaims:)

Lord Jesus,
You are king! You have come into our hearts, into our lives, into our world. There you reign as king for ever.

Make us worthy to live in your kingdom. Give us courage to serve you through serving your people.

Make us signs that your kingdom has already begun. We shout your praises as king for ever. Alleluia! Alleluia! Alleluia!

(Process with the crown as you place smaller crowns on the doors in your home.)

CYCLE C

Nov 20, 1983 / Nov 23, 1986 / Nov 26, 1989